The Getaway Guy

Road Trip Getaways with Mike O'Brian

Written By Mike O'Brian

www.thegetawayguy.com

Published by
Earthquake Company
www.EarthquakeGroup.com
Rochester, NY
© Copyright 2008

ISBN 978-0-615-17255-2

Printed in the United States of America
Design by Eric Skivington
www.SX2Design.com

The information in this book was accurate to the best of our knowledge at the time it was printed. Please check with individual organizations for the latest prices, hours, contact information, etc. They are subject to change.

Thank you for purchasing The Getaway Guy! This book was created to help you enjoy the great state of New York and the many wonderful destinations it has to offer. Please visit our website (www.thegetawaybook.com) for information on our next release as well as other useful info for your travels. Be safe and have fun!

The views expressed are solely those of the author and do not reflect the views of any of the sponsors or businesses affiliated with, or discussed, in this book.

Special thanks to:
Esperanza Mansion
Mercury Print Productions
Time Warner Cable
Walter Colley Images
R News
Capital News 9
News 10 Now
NY1

To my Mom and Dad who instilled in me as a kid the thrill of travel with road-trip vacations every summer. And to my daughter, Carly, and sister, Maureen who carry on the same sense of adventure. With all my love.

Mike O'Brian...The Getaway Guy!

Born in Corning, New York, Mike O'Brian began his broadcasting career in 1971 at Rochester radio station WSAY. Stations like WBBF and WVOR followed with a brief time in Tampa, Florida at WQXM radio. Mike's on-air experience in radio prepared him for his career in television. He joined RNEWS in 1995 for the  launch of its 24-hour news channel and is known for his TV travels around the state as The Getaway Guy.

"Travel has always been my passion and now I can bring all of my favorite getaways to viewers."

In addition to New York State getaways, Mike loves traveling the back roads of the New England Coast along with a week or two during the winter in the Caribbean. The American southwest is also a favorite destination. In between getaways, Mike devotes his years of commercial voice-over experience as president and director of The American Broadcasting Institute, his own broadcasting school designed to teach people how to break into the world of voice-over work.

There's not a lot of spare time left in a day, but when there is, Mike enjoys working in his back yard, entertaining friends and working off some occasional stress at the gym. Most of the time you'll find Mike behind the wheel, off on another road trip ready to enjoy his greatest passion.

"I get great satisfaction when people tell me how much they really enjoyed traveling to one of my recent getaways!"

Getaway Locations

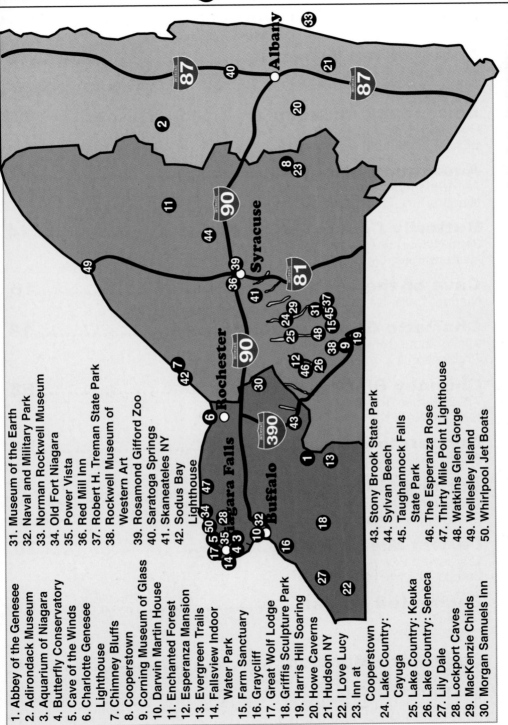

1. Abbey of the Genesee
2. Adirondack Museum
3. Aquarium of Niagara
4. Butterfly Conservatory
5. Cave of the Winds
6. Charlotte Genesee Lighthouse
7. Chimney Bluffs
8. Cooperstown
9. Corning Museum of Glass
10. Darwin Martin House
11. Enchanted Forest
12. Esperanza Mansion
13. Evergreen Trails
14. Fallsview Indoor Water Park
15. Farm Sanctuary
16. Graycliff
17. Great Wolf Lodge
18. Griffis Sculpture Park
19. Harris Hill Soaring
20. Howe Caverns
21. Hudson NY
22. I Love Lucy
23. Inn at Cooperstown
24. Lake Country: Cayuga
25. Lake Country: Keuka
26. Lake Country: Seneca
27. Lily Dale
28. Lockport Caves
29. MacKenzie Childs
30. Morgan Samuels Inn
31. Museum of the Earth
32. Naval and Military Park
33. Norman Rockwell Museum
34. Old Fort Niagara
35. Power Vista
36. Red Mill Inn
37. Robert H. Treman State Park
38. Rockwell Museum of Western Art
39. Rosamond Gifford Zoo
40. Saratoga Springs
41. Skaneateles NY
42. Sodus Bay Lighthouse
43. Stony Brook State Park
44. Sylvan Beach
45. Taughannock Falls State Park
46. The Esperanza Rose
47. Thirty Mile Point Lighthouse
48. Watkins Glen Gorge
49. Wellesley Island
50. Whirlpool Jet Boats

Table of Contents

Table of Contents

Table of Contents

The Getaway Guy: Road Trip Getaways with Mike O'Brian

Table of Contents

Map Key

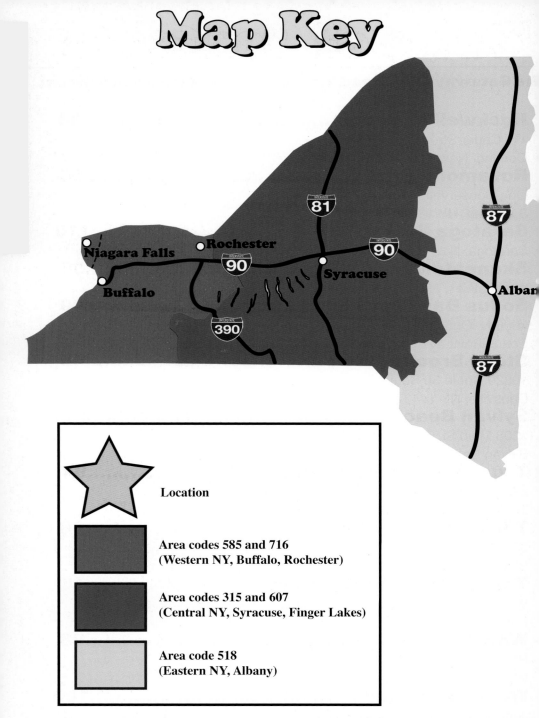

Location

Area codes 585 and 716
(Western NY, Buffalo, Rochester)

Area codes 315 and 607
(Central NY, Syracuse, Finger Lakes)

Area code 518
(Eastern NY, Albany)

Look for the large orange star on each color coded destination. Then look at the zoomed in area and find the small orange star. This, along with the Gettin' There directions provided, will point you in the right direction. Mapquest.com and Google.com are great resources that can give you accurate driving directions from your home address.

Getaway Icon Key

Icons	Meaning
	Couples
	Family
	Great for Animal Lovers
	Bring Your Camera!
	Open Seasonally
	Prepare to Get Wet!
	Dining Available
	Lodging
	Historical

Abbey of the Genesee
PIFFARD, NY

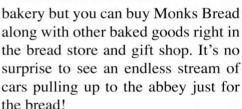

If you're in need of a quiet place to rest and reflect, this getaway may be just right for you. The 'Abbey of the Genesee', just outside of the town of Piffard, is home to several monks carrying on the monastic way of life in Livingston County. It is open to the public.

The monks welcome visitors to join the community for liturgical prayer in the beautiful Abbey Church. But before you head that way, the reception room's large selection of spiritual books will catch your attention. Your sense of smell will play a big part of your visit here too. The aroma of Monks Bread is everywhere! In order for the monks to support themselves, the business of baking bread is a daily routine in their enormous, immaculate baking facility. You won't be able to tour the bakery but you can buy Monks Bread along with other baked goods right in the bread store and gift shop. It's no surprise to see an endless stream of cars pulling up to the abbey just for the bread!

Because this is a cloistered monastery, there are no tours of the facility. A porter is available to answer questions and provide assistance. Many people come here just for the solitude on the grounds or in the church. Some even spend a week or weekend at one of their three retreat homes just up the road, Bethlehem, Bethany and Nazareth. Each one is situated within a wooded area providing plenty of space for walks and quiet time. A rather serious silence is maintained throughout the retreats. The cost is $45 per person / per night.

"If you're in need of a quiet place to rest and reflect, this getaway may be just right for you."

Travel Tip...

Lunch? You're close enough to the town of Geneseo that has plenty of restaurants to choose from including the famous Big Tree Inn.

ADMISSION: FREE!

GETTIN' THERE...

5 miles West of Geneseo, 35 miles South of Rochester. From 390, exit #8 at Geneseo then West on Route 20A. Pick up Route 63 North to River Road in Piffard. Look for the sign to the Abbey.

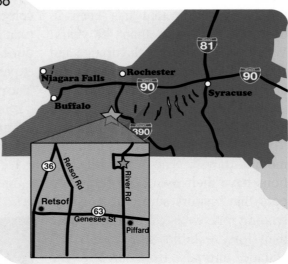

CONTACT...

Hours: 2am-7pm, Bookstore is open throughout the day. Bread Store 8am-7pm.
Call: (585) 243-0660, Retreat House (585) 243-2220
Visit: www.geneseeabbey.org

Aquarium of Niagara
NIAGARA FALLS, NY

Sharks may have taken a back seat to a clownfish at "The Aquarium of Niagara", a family attraction that has been in operation for more than 40 years! When youngsters spot the orange and white fish in one of the many colorful tanks, they yell the name Nemo!

The sharks in the new shark exhibit are pretty impressive too. You'll even see a few relics from the movie "Jaws". The California sea lions have their own 100,000 gallon pool that visitors surround to watch feeding time every 90 minutes. More than forty exhibits showcase 1,500 aquatic animals from around the globe including Moray eels, piranhas and Peruvian penguins.

Outside of New York City, Aquarium of Niagara is New York State's only indoor aquarium, perfect for a family day trip when in the Niagara Falls region. Expect to spend about two hours.

≫ Looking for a special way to celebrate your birthday? You can plan a once in a lifetime opportunity during an after hour birthday experience, aquarium style!

Your party includes:
- *Touch tank session.*
- *Pizza, cake, and drinks.*
- *A special sea lion show.*
- *Access to all exhibits.*
- *Ages 8 and up - Your choice of a seal, sea lion, or penguin encounter.*

"The sharks in the new exhibit are pretty impressive too!"

ATTRACTION...

Wanna feed a Seal? For $5, kids and adults can feed Pacific and Atlantic Harbor Seals from the public area of the outdoor pool. It's a once in a lifetime experience! (seasonal)

ADMISSION: Adults $9.00, Children (4-12) $6.00, 3 and under free, Seniors (60+) $5.50

GETTIN' THERE...

Take the NYS Thruway West to Buffalo. Pick up Route 290 West to Route 190 North. After the 2nd bridge take the Robert Moses Parkway (exit #21) to the 'city traffic' exit which will take you into Niagara Falls. Follow John B. Daly Blvd. to the end and turn left onto Niagara Street. Go down 2 stoplights and turn right onto Third Street. The Aquarium is down 3 blocks on your left.

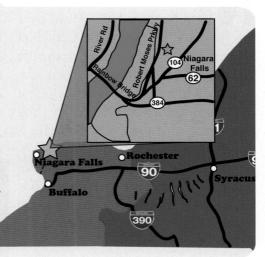

CONTACT...

Hours: Open everyday from 9am to 5 pm, year round (excluding Thanksgiving and Christmas Day).
Call: 1-800-500-4609 or **Visit:** www.aquariumofniagara.org

Butterfly Conservatory
NIAGARA FALLS, CANADA

Mother nature has her beautiful work on display in Niagara Falls. Head over the Rainbow Bridge to the Canadian side, North on River Rd. along the Niagara River to the Niagara Parks Botanical Gardens. This is the home of the Butterfly Conservatory and also home to over 2000 butterflies, open year-round.

Expect to see a tropical paradise filled with magnificent butterflies in-flight all around you in an 11,000 square foot enclosed conservatory. Paths wind through the rainforest setting, past a pond and waterfall and the Emergence Window, where butterflies leave their pupae and prepare to take their first flight!

After the Butterfly Conservatory, check out the unbelievable gardens! The Botanical Gardens cover much of the park displaying all kinds of flora during spring and summer months.

Also, if you're looking for more than a snack bar to satisfy your hunger, you can head into Niagara On the Lake, just a few miles north, for an endless choice of restaurants and bakeries.

Bring your camera! The photo ops are endless here.

Dinner time for the butterflies!

"Expect to see a tropical paradise filled with magnificent butterflies."

Travel Tip...

Even though this tropical get-away makes sense in the colder months, the biggest crowds and longer waiting periods actually occur in the summer!

ADMISSION: $11 Adults, $6.50 Children (6-12), 5 and under are free. Prices are in Canadian dollars plus tax.

Gettin' There...

From the NYS Thruway tollbooth in Buffalo, take the first exit, Rt. 290 West to Rt. 190 North/Niagara Falls. After the 2nd bridge get onto the Robert Moses Parkway exit #21 into Niagara Falls and over The Rainbow Bridge to the Canadian side. Continue to take right turns until you come to River Road. Go left and follow the Niagara River. You'll find the Botanical Gardens and the Butterfly Conservatory about 3 miles up on your left.

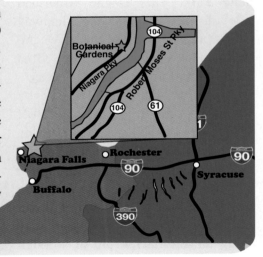

Contact...

Hours: Open year round (except Dec. 25th). Open daily at 9am. Closing times vary from 5pm to 9pm depending on time of year.
Call: (905) 356-8119 or **Visit:** www.niagaraparks.com

Cave of the Winds
NIAGARA FALLS, NY

Cave of the Winds can be found in one of America's oldest parks, Niagara Falls State Park. This is the American side of the falls and the Getaway Guy's favorite because the views are spectacular! Get yourself onto Goat Island to find this exciting getaway.

Cave of the Winds begins by taking you on a journey 175 feet deep into the Niagara Gorge via underground elevator to the bottom of the falls. You'll walk through a tunnel and appear at the base where the American Falls come crashing down as you eventually find your way along an intricate set-up of wooden walkways.

Hard to believe, but the walkways are torn down and rebuilt every year! Mother nature replaces the structure with about 70 feet of ice buildup where the walkways stand in the Spring, Summer and Fall.

If you've ever seen the 1953 movie 'Niagara', you'll recognize this area. It's where Marilyn Monroe did much of her filming. The same tacky yellow ponchos are used today to keep you dry. The mandatory canvas footwear adds to the Cave of the Winds fashion statement!

If your around after dark, the best place to get a fantastic view of the illuminated falls is at nearby Prospect Point!

Mike braves the hurricane deck!

"Hold on! Only the brave choose to walk the Hurricane Deck!"

ATTRACTION...

Hold on! Only the brave choose to walk the Hurricane Deck, only 20 feet away from Bridal Veil Falls where winds can reach up to 70 mph!

ADMISSION: $10 Adults, $7 (6-12), 5 and under are free but must be at least 42 inches tall.

GETTIN' THERE...

After the NYS Thruway toll booths in Buffalo, take exit #50, Rt. 290 West to the Rt. 190 North/Niagara Falls exit. After crossing the 2nd bridge, take your 1st exit (exit #21) to the Robert Moses Parkway. The parkway turns into Prospect St. Signs will direct you to parking. Lot #2 will put you closest to the attraction.

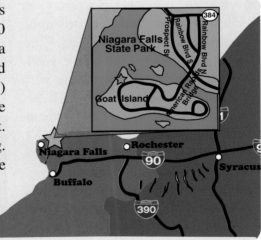

CONTACT...

Hours: April-December (April-May 9am-4:45pm, May-June 9am-9pm, July-Aug. 9am-10pm, Sept.-Oct. 9am-8pm, Oct-Dec. 9am -4:45pm).
Call: (716) 282-1730 or **Visit:** www.niagarafallsstatepark.com

Charlotte-Genesee Lighthouse
ROCHESTER, NY

How about a walk into history? You can literally do that on this Getaway in Rochester, New York. Surprisingly, you may have passed by The Charlotte-Genesee Lighthouse without even knowing it! Hard to see with so much built around it now but it's been right there off of Lake Avenue in the village of Charlotte since 1822. The U.S. Government declared the entire lighthouse site a surplus property in 1981. After being turned over to the newly formed Charlotte-Genesee Lighthouse Historical Society, renovations began in 1983.

The lighthouse came close to being destroyed. In the mid '60's, students from Charlotte High School and Edison Tech were responsible for keeping the lighthouse in one piece. The Coast guard helped with a new light and she stands today near Ontario Beach Park. The museum next to the lighthouse is small but very important to its past.

Today, the lighthouse is a fantastic trip back into local history for lighthouse enthusiasts with tours given by knowledgeable volunteers.

Restored by the Lighthouse Historical Society in 1984.

"The lighthouse is a fantastic trip back into local history."

Travel Tip...

If you want to get to the top of the tower, get ready to climb the 42-step spiral staircase followed by an 11-foot ladder! Kids have to be at least 4 feet tall and no floppy shoes! The view is great! »

ADMISSION: There is no charge but donations are gladly accepted. Museum is handicap accessible.

GETTIN' THERE...

Follow Lake Avenue north from downtown Rochester, New York. As you get closer to Lake Ontario in Charlotte, turn right onto Lighthouse Street. The lighthouse is behind Holy Cross Church. Free parking.

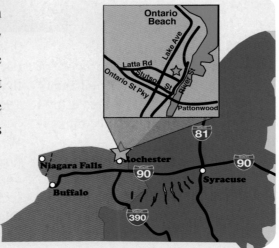

CONTACT...

Hours: Early-May through the end of October, Saturdays and Sundays from 1pm to 5pm. Groups are welcome any day by appointment.
Call: (585) 621-6179 or **Visit:** www.geneseelighthouse.org

Darwin Martin House

BUFFALO, NY

"Frank Lloyd Wright designed more than 1000 projects!" »

This is a getaway to a residential neighborhood of Buffalo, NY, in Erie County to discover one of Frank Lloyd Wright's most treasured compositions.

Designed and built between 1903 and 1905, the Darwin D. Martin House is located at 125 Jewitt Parkway. It has just gone through a major restoration and the complex, comprised of many buildings, is open to the public.

The Martin House was the home of Isabelle and Darwin Martin, an area entrepreneur. After selecting architect Frank Lloyd Wright to design the property, the two men became close friends, a friendship that lasted until Martin's death in 1935.

The Martin House ranks among Wright's greatest and important projects from Wright's Prairie School era. Walking inside gives you the feeling of being closed in at first then released into a large open space. It happens throughout the tour intentionally. This was one of Wright's signature design concepts.

If you're an admirer of Frank Lloyd Wright, be sure to check out the excellent gift shop next door.

"The Martin house ranks among Wright's greatest and important projects."

Travel Tip...

The Gardener's Cottage has rarely been seen by the public until now on In-Depth and Focus Tours only. Call ahead! These longer tours have higher admission fees.

> **ADMISSION:** Adults $15.00 Students $10.00 Seniors $13.00. Reservations for all tours are a must! Basic tours last an hour.

GETTIN' THERE...

Follow the NYS Thruway to Buffalo. After the toll, continue on I- 90 to the Rt. 33 West exit. Take this to Rt. 198 West and exit onto Parkside Ave. Head North 4 blocks and a right turn onto Jewitt Parkway. You can park on the street at 125 Jewitt Parkway.

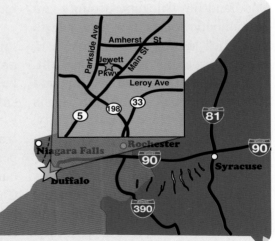

CONTACT...

Hours: Open year round-Tours everyday except Tuesday.
Call: (716) 856-3858 or **Visit:** www.darwinmartinhouse.org

Evergreen Trails
ANGELICA, NY

I f you're looking to getaway from it all, Evergreen Trails Campground may fit the bill. Secluded within 211 acres of woodland in Allegany County are 25 authentic log cabins available to rent. Each accommodation has heat, stove, refrigerator and sleeping loft. Renters bring their own bedding and cooking supplies. Evergreen Trails supplies the seclusion and serenity. Cabins range in size and design accommodating from 2 to 8 people.

Two centralized bathhouses come equipped with four separate bathrooms with shower, sink and toilet. Very private! Showers and laundry facilities are coin-operated.

There are also a variety of open or wooded sites for tents, trailers and RV's with electricity, picnic tables and campfire rings. The grounds have a picnic pavilion, recreation hall with video arcade games, camp store with firewood and ice, volleyball, basketball and a children's playground. Even Saturday afternoon hay rides. Leashed pets are welcome.

I like the large separation between log cabins for privacy. For large groups or families that may want to be together, there are close groups of smaller cabins set in a loop.

So, if you need to get away from the daily routine and yearn for peace and quiet with a large dose of nature, head to Evergreen Trails Campground. This may be the best-kept secret in the southern tier! And it's one great Getaway!

"This may be the best-kept secret in the southern tier!"

Travel Tip...

Bring your fishing pole! There are two private ponds for catch and release! Also, you're only a few miles away from the quaint little town of Angelica, N.Y., home to many antique shops!

ADMISSION: Cabins range from $65 to $115 per night, plus tax. Campsites range from $23-$26.

GETTIN' THERE...

Route 390 in the southern tier to Exit # 7 / Mount Morris. Pick up Route 408 South to Nunda. Turn right onto Route 436 West and proceed 3 miles to Livingston County Rd. 20 (Short Tract Road). Head South 15 miles to Evergreen Trails.

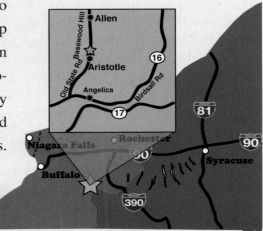

CONTACT...

Call: (585) 466-7993 for reservations.
Visit: www.evergeentrails.com

fallsview Indoor Water Park
NIAGARA FALLS, CANADA

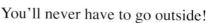

You won't have to fly all the way to Florida to find summertime fun this winter. Once you cross the Rainbow Bridge into Niagara Falls, Canada, you'll notice that the skyline has changed. Sitting high atop the public parking garage behind the Brock Plaza Hotel is the fantastic 8-story high Fallsview Indoor Water Park!

At a constant 84 degrees inside, you'll have sixteen thrilling water slides to choose from, some up to six stories high! There's also a giant wave pool, two oversized adult-only Jacuzzis and a Tiny Tots Splash Park.

Spending the night in Niagara Falls? Consider one of three hotels connected to the water park: Sheraton On The Falls, the historic Brock Plaza Hotel and the Skyline Inn.

You'll never have to go outside!

If you get water-logged but still need some excitement, you can literally walk on over to famous Clifton Hill. You'll find a high concentration of touristy fun from wax museums to haunted houses. The Sky Wheel is the new attraction here that gives you the best view of the falls from high, high above. The wheel's cars are all heated, so any time of year is great. In fact, all of Clifton Hill's attractions are open all year round!

"A constant 84 degrees inside the park at all times!"

Travel Tip...

Check out the Fallsview Water Park web site for package deals. At $44.95 per person for water park admission, an overnight stay at one of the connecting hotels including passes in the price could save your family money. **Don't forget your passport!**

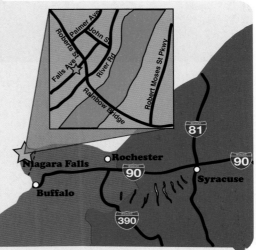

ADMISSION: $44.95 per person plus tax (Canadian dollars), Walk-Ins allowed.

GETTIN' THERE...

NYS Thruway to Buffalo. Pick up exit #50 to route 290 West. Then onto the route 190 North exit. Take the Robert Moses Parkway (exit #21) until you see the 'city traffic' exit. This will take you into Niagara Falls. Cross the Rainbow Bridge into Canada and continue straight up the hill. A left turn onto Falls Avenue will take you to the parking ramps. An elevator ride to the top takes you to the water park!

CONTACT...

Hours: Open year round, as early as 9am and as late as 10pm. See web site for detailed hours. (some dates subject to change)
Call: 1-800-263-7135 or **Visit:** www.fallsviewwaterpark.com

Grayeliff

DERBY, NY

If you've ever visited the Darwin Martin House in Buffalo, N.Y., the logical thing to do is to see the Martin's summer home in Derby, N.Y., just south of Buffalo. In 1926, on the cliffs overlooking Lake Erie, American master architect Frank Lloyd Wright designed Graycliff for the wife of Darwin Martin.

Isabelle's eyesight was failing and she directed Mr. Wright to create structures full of sunlight and air. He fulfilled her wishes magnificently with broadly cantilevered balconies that opened the building to soft lake air. Ribbons of glass windows and doors let in the sunlight. In fact you can actually see directly through the house because of this design. Signature Frank Lloyd Wright details carry through the 6,500 square-foot home that you can tour today.

Find wall-to-wall Frank Lloyd Wright in the very extensive gift shop. The items are unique and of high quality. Frank wouldn't have it any other way!

>> *"Signature Frank Lloyd Wright details carry through the sixty-five hundred square foot home."*

Travel Tip...

Tour guides are extremely knowledgeable. Be sure to ask them about Frank Lloyd Wright's surprise visit to Graycliff only months before he died!

> **ADMISSION:** $15 per person, 21 and younger $10, **RESERVATIONS are a must!**

GETTIN' THERE...

Follow the NY State Thruway West to exit #57 (Hamburg/Camp Road/Rt.75). After tolls, go right onto Camp Rd. (Rt. 75 north) then a left onto Southwestern Blvd./US Rt. 20. Follow this for 5.6 miles then right onto South Creek Rd. Go left onto Old Lake Shore Rd. to Graycliff on your right.

CONTACT...

Hours: April-November with limited winter hours.
Call: (716) 947-9217 or **Visit:** www.graycliff.bfn.org

Great Wolf Lodge
NIAGARA FALLS, CANADA

Imagine pulling up to a four-story, log-sided resort on a 25-acre site that has more than 400 all-suite guest rooms, restaurants, spa, shops, gym and..... a 103,000 square foot indoor water park! This Canadian Getaway has all of this and more.

Great Wolf Lodge is drawing families from all over the region. It's easy to get to just by heading to Niagara Falls and crossing the Rainbow Bridge into Canada. Head north along the Niagara Parkway onto Victoria Avenue and you're there!

This getaway makes a lot of sense especially in the middle of winter. You could literally spend your stay in your flip-flops and bathing suit because you never have to leave the resort. Everything you need is in one place. Kids love the animated animals in the living room lobby and moms and dads love the comfort and family-like setting.

Everyone loves the 13 water slides at 'Bear Track Landing'. This 90-foot tall, mountain-themed water park has a giant wave pool, outdoor adult only hot spa, locker rooms with showers and swimsuit dryers and snack bars. And it's always a very warm 84 degrees! The indoor water park is exclusive to resort guests only with passes included with your overnight accommodations.

So, if you're looking for a great place to escape the cold and you don't want to get on a plane, head north to Great Wolf Lodge. A perfect getaway for the whole family!

There are eleven Great Wolf Lodge locations in North America.

> ## *"You never have to leave the resort. Everything you need is in one place."*

Travel Tip...

If you're at the lodge during the holiday season in December, take a ride back down near the falls on the Niagara Parkway for the annual Festival of Lights. You can drive by 3 or more miles of breathtaking holiday lights including two parks off the main route. And it's all free!

> **ADMISSION:** **$199-$599 per night (Canadian dollars). Visitors get 2 days of play with a 1-night stay. Go to their web site for reservations and promotions.**

GETTIN' THERE...

NYS Thruway to Buffalo. Pick up exit #50 to Route 290 West. Then onto the Route 190 North exit. Take the Robert Moses Parkway (exit #21) until you see the 'city traffic' exit. This will take you into Niagara Falls. Cross the Rainbow Bridge into Canada and continue straight and up the hill. Follow the Falls sign to your right and a left onto River Rd. to Great Wolf Lodge.

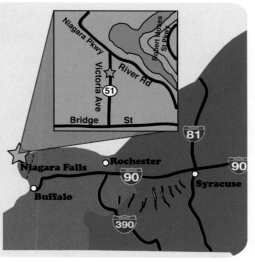

CONTACT...

Hours: Open year round.
Call: (905) 354-4888 for information, 1-888-878-1818 for reservations.
Visit: www.greatwolf.com

Griffis Sculpture Park

EAST OTTO, NY

"Climbing on many ⌃ of the sculptures is encouraged!"

Climbing on giant insects in the middle of a park isn't something you do everyday, but you can do it when you visit Griffis Sculpture Park in Cattaraugus County. Expect to see giant sculptures of insects and animals plus towers and castles scattered over 400 acres of ponds, meadows, hills and trails. This park takes art and nature and puts them together for all to enjoy. This is truly a unique experience for kids and adults alike.

Here's one thing that some people don't know. Griffis Sculpture Park is actually two distinct places: the Mill Valley site and the Rohr Hill site.

Only 1.5 miles separate the parks, a very easy five-minute ride.

The Ashford Hollow Foundation was founded in 1966 by artist Larry W. Griffis, Jr., who is responsible for the alien-like sculptures found in one side of the park. The other nearby location has more current works from local, national and international artists. The park is a wildlife preserve. Pack out what you have packed in. No pets allowed.

Map information and an honor box for the $5 adult admission can be found at the park's entrance near the parking lot.

"This park takes art and nature and puts them together for all to enjoy!"

Travel Tip...

Here's an idea! After you've spent time at the park, continue south on Rt. 219 into the 19th Century town of Ellicottville, N.Y. for great shops and restaurants! You're only a half-hour away!

ADMISSION: $5.00 for the honor box.

Gettin' There...

I-90 West through Buffalo to Route 219 South (Orchard Park) into the hamlet of Ashford Hollow. Look for signs to Griffis Sculpture Park at Ahrens Road. You will go up a big hill to a 'Y' in the road. If you go left onto Rohr Hill Road, the Rohr Hill site is 1/2 mile down the road. Continue further down Rohr Hill Rd and take a right onto Mill Valley Rd. This will take you to the Mill Valley site.

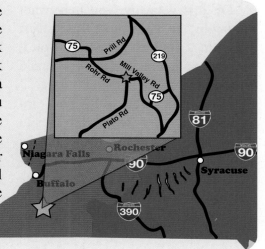

Contact...

Hours: May 1 - October 31, dawn to dusk.
Call: (716) 667-2808 or **Visit:** www.griffispark.org

I love lucy

JAMESTOWN, NY

From 69 Stewart Avenue, her birthplace, to Lake View Cemetery, her resting place, Jamestown, New York is all about Lucille Ball.

On this getaway, you may want to begin at the new Lucy-Desi Museum at 10 West 3rd Street. You'll find unique interactive exhibits and a lot of Lucy and Desi memorabilia.

Just up the street at #2 West 3rd Street, be sure to stop in the Desilu Playhouse. That's the name of the studio 'I Love Lucy' was filmed at. Here, there are exact replicas of the Ricardos' New York City apartment. There's even a Vitameatavegamin opportunity here!

Don't miss the huge Lucy-Desi Center Gift Shop right across the street at 300 North Main St.

Lucy's childhood homes can be seen here in town. Her birthplace is at 69 Stewart Ave. and she grew up at 59 Lucy Lane in Celoron. (Both are now private residences so please respect their privacy). Even Lucy's grave site can be seen at Lake View Cemetery at 907 Lakeview Avenue. Lucy's ashes are interred with her parents and other Hunt family members. Enter the cemetery from Buffalo St. and Lakeview Ave. Go straight through the main gate and take your first right turn. Just up a bit, look for a small arrow on a square stone that leads you to her burial site. There is a pathway that leads to the head stone. You can't miss it.

Maps and directions to all Lucy locations are available at the Lucy Museum and the Desilu Playhouse. If you love Lucy, you'll love Jamestown, New York. Pretty much, everywhere you go in town, it's hard to forget why you're there. It's all about Lucy!

"Unique interactive exhibits and a lot of Lucy and Desi memorabilia."

Travel Tip...

There are two annual festivals in town celebrating the first couple of comedy. Check their website for scheduled dates.

BIRTHPLACE OF
LUCILLE BALL
AUGUST 6, 1911 – APRIL 26, 1989
FIRST LADY OF COMEDY
PLACED BY HISTORICAL MARKER COMMITTEE
AND ARTS COUNCIL FOR
CHAUTAUQUA COUNTY

ADMISSION: Desilu Playhouse: $10 Adults, $9 Seniors, Youths (6-18) $7. Lucy-Desi Museum: $6 Adults, $5 Seniors, Youths (6-18) $4. You can obtain a dual-admission for both the museum and playhouse.

GETTIN' THERE...

NYS Thruway West toward Erie, PA. exit #59 Dunkirk-Fredonia. Follow Route 60 South to Jamestown.

From the Southern Tier, follow I-86 West to exit #12. Then Route 60 South to Jamestown.

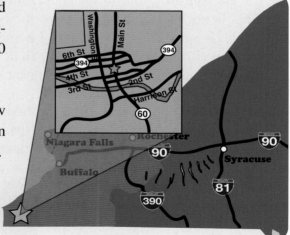

CONTACT...

Hours: Museum & Playhouse open Monday - Saturday 10 a.m. to 5:30 p.m.and Sunday 1-5 p.m. (Closed some major holidays)
Call: 1-877-LUCY-FAN (582-9326)
Visit: www.lucy-desi.com

Lily Dale

LILY DALE, NY

magine driving along a scenic road along the ridge of a beautiful lake and approaching a white booth where you'll pay an admission fee for the gate to go up to let you in. This is not the drive-in. This is Lily Dale, a spiritualist community outside the village of Cassadaga in Chautauqua County.

Among gingerbread houses on quaint neighborhood streets, there's something quite unique beyond the restaurants and parks by the lake. Look closer to find working mediums and demonstrations on clairvoyance, meditation and healings in The Healing Temple, thought exchange evenings, workshops and lectures from top names in the field of spiritualism. There are two hotels on the property plus a number of bed and breakfasts.

There is great history here. This has been going on in Lily Dale for 125 years!

Medium's donations start at $40 and can be arranged in advance or scheduled the day of your visit. Look for a clipboard outside most medium's homes to see when they might be able to fit you in. Price and quality are not necessarily related. (see website)

Add your name to the list of thousands that have been here including Susan B. Anthony and Franklin & Eleanor Roosevelt. Even Mae West was here!

"There's something quite unique beyond the restaurants and parks by the lake!"

Travel Tip...

Come to Lily Dale with good walking shoes AND an open mind. Expect to visit a community of friendly people who live and work here.

ADMISSION: $10 per person / 24-Hour Pass, $5 per person 6pm-12 Midnight, 18 or younger free with adult. Tours available through the office.

GETTIN' THERE...

From the NYS Thruway, exit #59 to NY Route 60 South. Drive 8 miles and turn right onto Dale Drive in the village of Cassadaga. Go one mile to the Lily Dale entrance gate. Lily Dale is one hour south of Buffalo, N.Y.

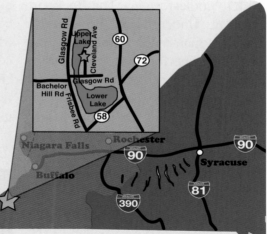

CONTACT...

Hours: Last day of June through the day before Labor Day.
Call: (716) 595-8721 or (716) 595-2505
Visit: www.lilydaleassembly.com

Lockport Caves
LOCKPORT, NY

If all that fun in the summer sun has you looking for a bit of relief, check out Lockport, New York's 'coolest' tour... The Lockport Cave & Underground Boat Ride! This is a man-made tunnel from the 1800's meant for tons of water to power factories 50 feet above. Today, it's 'a cave tour' that takes you on the same path the water took years ago. Add lights, a boat and a few able-bodied tour guides and you've got an excellent one-hour tour within an engineering marvel.

The tour begins outdoors as you explore the historic Erie Canal Locks 67-71. Then it's a walk below the earth through an enormous water tunnel that was blasted out of solid rock in the 1850's. The underground boat ride comes at the end of the tour.

Grab a sweater or sweatshirt since it's always about 55 degrees down below. Good walking shoes are a must too. The tour does supply rain coats for the 'wet' part of the tour. My suggestion is to skip the clammy covering and 'tough it out'. Bring a camera! So if you're looking for a fun day-trip getaway with a bit of history, try "Lockport Caves" in Lockport, New York. A great way to stay 'cooool' this Summer!

"An excellent one-hour tour within an engineering marvel!"

Travel Tip...

Come October, there's a lot of screaming coming from down below! The annual Lockport Haunted Cave is a very popular Halloween tour! Call for reservations. (716) 438-0174.

**Not a lot of light »
down here!**

ADMISSION: Adults $9, Children (4-12) $6. All prices plus tax. There are deals with AAA, AARP, Student Discount, Military, Group rates.

GETTIN' THERE...

NYS Thruway to exit #48A (Pembroke). Take Rt. 77 North (it's more scenic than Rt. 78) all the way into Lockport, N.Y. Careful! Rt. 77 winds and curves and changes direction a few times. Once in town, look for Pine Street, take a right and look for the stone building on your right at the bridge.

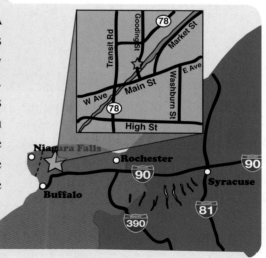

CONTACT...

Hours: Daily from 2nd week of May through October 31st. Tours are hourly from 12pm in the Spring, from 10am in Summer and from 11am in the Fall. Weekends only in early Spring. Check web site for complete operating hours.
Call: (716) 438-0174 or **Visit:** www.lockportcave.com

Morgan Samuels Inn
CANANDAIGUA, NY

"Morgan Samuels is among the most distinctive Inns of North America!"

»

There's nothing like hanging out in front of a nice cozy fireplace when it's cold and snowy outside. But if one fireplace isn't enough, try eleven! That's how many there are at The Morgan Samuels Inn, Smith Road in Canandaigua, New York. Wood burning and English coal grate fireplaces can be found in most of the rooms at this historic mansion situated on 46 acres of fields, woods and creek.

Six guest rooms are available for overnight stays, five of which have their own fireplace. A candlelit breakfast is included with your stay. Dinners are by reservation with a minimum of 8 guests attending.

According to Discerning Traveler Magazine, The Morgan Samuels Inn has been recognized as one of the 12 most romantic hideaways in the east! Once inside, you'll see why! It's my choice for a cozy wintertime getaway. And in the fall, you're close enough to the Finger Lakes and its wineries to make it a great autumn getaway.

"One of the twelve most romantic getaways in the East!"

Travel Tip...

Request either the Morgan Suite or the Victorian Room. Both have king beds, great views and a Jacuzzi! Both are popular so reserve early!

ADMISSION: Ranging from $119 to $295 depending on the room and time of year. There is a 2-night minimum stay on Friday / Saturday from mid-May through mid-November. No Children under 12. There is restricted smoking and no pets allowed.

GETTIN' THERE...

From Interstate 90 (NYS Thruway) take exit #43 and head South on Route 332, through downtown Canandaigua. Go left onto routes 5 & 20 heading East. Take a left turn onto County Road 10 to the blinking light. Turn right and proceed a ½ mile and look for the entrance to the driveway.

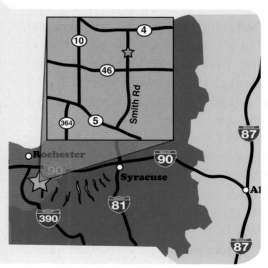

CONTACT...

Hours: Open year round (closed Christmas eve/day).
Call: (585) 394-9232 or **Visit:** www.morgansamuelsinn.com

Naval & Military Park
BUFFALO, NY

As if we didn't have enough patriotism in us these days! Head to the "Naval & Military Park" in downtown Buffalo, New York and you'll get more. I did. Not only another blast of patriotism but a true appreciation for what our dads, uncles and grandfathers went through during World War II.

The first ship you'll see resting in the waters of Lake Erie is the cruiser "USS Little Rock". The main attraction here is the national historic landmark "USS The Sullivans", named after the 5 Sullivan brothers who all lost their lives on "The Juneau" in World War II.

Both ships offer several antiquated rooms and passageways that you will have the chance to explore and sense the way it might have felt being on-board.

Military equipment like the UH-1 "Huey" helicopter, the M-41 "Walker Bulldog" Tank and the "Voodoo", the popular F-101 aircraft, can be found just outside the indoor museum. The kids will enjoy a ride on the flight simulator!

This Getaway is affordable so the the whole family can go. For me, it brought a great deal of history and a truer appreciation of the sacrifices made in World War II. It will for you too. It's well-worth the drive! The tours are self-guided and take about 2-hours. You can call in advance for a complete guided tour.

> *"A true appreciation for what our dads, uncles and grandfathers went through during WWII."*

Travel Tip...

Be sure to talk with the guides who handle the tours. Most of them have been in the war and they know what it was like. They are a very important element to your experience on this getaway.

ADMISSION: Adults $8, Ages 6-16 and Seniors $5, Under 6 free. Limited handicap accessibility.

GETTIN' THERE...

Head toward Buffalo, N.Y. on The NYS Thruway. Pay the toll and get onto Route 190 North into down-town Buffalo. Look for Exit #53, Church Street then follow the signs to "The Naval & Military Park". Park in the lot at the corner of Marine Dr. and Erie St.

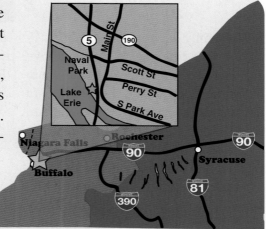

CONTACT...

Hours: 7 Days a Week, 10am-5pm, April through October. Weekends in November.

Call: (716) 847-1773 Ext. 10 or **Visit:** www.buffalonavalpark.org

Old Fort Niagara

YOUNGSTOWN, NY

"Make sure to catch the amazing reenactments throughout the summer months!" »

Family day trip of fun and facts! Standing on a bluff above Lake Ontario not far from Niagara Falls, Old Fort Niagara dominates the entrance to the Niagara River in the U.S.A.. It has been since 1726! Its history and wide open spaces make it a great family getaway.

Red coats and characters on-site keep the kids amused. The military architecture and 18th century fortifications will amaze mom and dad. Visitors have free reign of the grounds complete with rest rooms and snack bar. Fort Niagara is a New York State Historic Site that welcomes more than 100,000 visitors each year.

Expect to spend about 2 hours to see it all. Some of the major events during the summer months include:

Old Fort Niagara French & Indian War Encampment with 1000 Living History demonstrators gathering to depict the 1759 Siege of Niagara.
The War of 1812 Encampment.
Soldiers of the Revolution. British loyalist and native forces are pitted against continentals and frontier militia.

So, if you're heading to Niagara Falls this summer, why not take the road less traveled and discover something new at Old Fort Niagara!

"The history and wide open spaces make it a great family getaway!"

ATTRACTION...

Hold your ears! Ka Boom! Kids get to volunteer to help with the cannon demonstration.

Travel Tip...

If you are in the area to spend the night, there are many choices in the beautiful town Niagara on the Lake. You can see it from the fort but you have to travel back around to get to the Canadian side.

ADMISSION: Adults $10, (6-12) $6, (under 6) are free. AAA and Senior Citizen discounts.

GETTIN' THERE...

N.Y.S. Thruway to Buffalo onto exit #50. Follow I-290 West to I-190 North to exit #25B. Follow the Robert Moses Parkway North. Almost at the end of the parkway you will see the exit for Old Fort Niagara. Follow signs through the state park.

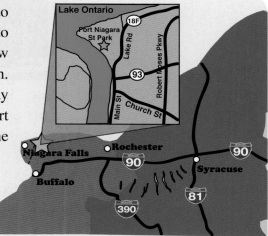

CONTACT...

Hours: Open all year, daily at 9am. Closing times vary from 4:30pm to 7:30pm. Closed Jan. 1, U.S. Thanksgiving Day and Christmas Day.

Call: 1-716-745-7611 or **Visit:** www.oldfortniagara.org

Power Vista
LEWISTON, NY

"See for miles from way above on the observation deck!"

SAFETY FIRST
DO NOT THROW OBJECTS FROM THE DECK PEOPLE WORKING BELOW

New York's biggest energy producer is also a great getaway!

The largest electric generating facility in Lewiston, New York is one of the largest in the United States. 4 1/2 miles downstream from Niagara Falls, the Niagara Project transforms the energy of the Niagara River into some of the nation's cleanest and least expensive electricity.

With more than 50 hands-on interactive displays, giant maps, movies and jaw-dropping views from the observation deck, this getaway is perfect for the whole family. School trips too!

Look for the beautifully restored seven-foot-high mural by American painter Thomas Hart Benton that depicts Father Louis Hennepin and a group of Native Americans viewing Niagara Falls during the priest's 17th century expedition in the New World. The mural was commissioned by the Power Authority when the Niagara project was built.

"New York's largest electric generating facility."

You are only minutes away from America's oldest park! Niagara Falls State Park!

ADMISSION: Parking and admission are always free! Handicap-accessible.

GETTIN' THERE...

I-90 NYS Thruway to Buffalo, then onto I-290 via exit #50 toward Niagara Falls. Merge onto I-190 toward Grand Island. Take exit #25A (Lewiston) Turn left onto Rt. 265 (Military Rd.) then another left onto Rt. 104 West. Turn left at the blinking yellow light. Entrance is on the left.

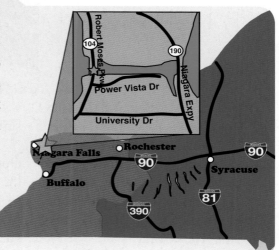

CONTACT...

Hours: Open year round 9am-5pm. Closed only on Thanksgiving, Christmas and New Years Day.
Call: New York Power Authority / Power Vista (716) 286-6661
Visit: www.nypa.gov/vc/niagara.htm

Stony Brook State Park

DANSVILLE, NY

"In winter three miles of cross-country trails are available for skiers!"

Afamily getaway all in a day! Thanks to Mother Nature's creative work over the past million years, water and glaciers have carved out an amazing spectacle over 577 acres in Livingston County. You'll find Stony Brook near Dansville, New York.

With waterfalls, hiking trails and endless natural beauty, the park is very 'user friendly'. Families with small children seem to be at ease with how safely the kids can play in the streams and pools. Of course with any outdoor setting like this, supervision is still essential.

There are three main waterfalls along the Gorge Trail. Second Fall is the most popular allowing everyone to get up close to this natural wonder. The stream-fed pool has varying depths for all ages and has lifeguard supervision.

Stony Brook has picnic pavilions, picnic areas with tables and grills, snack bar, large playground, tennis courts and play fields. For campers, there are 125 non-electric sites.

"Water and glaciers have carved out an amazing spectacle!"

Travel Tip...

Plan your trip to the park to coincide with the annual Festival of Balloons in Dansville over the Labor Day Weekend! **www.nysfob.com**

ADMISSION: $7 per car at park entrance.

GETTIN' THERE...

Take I-390 in Livingston County to exit #4, Dansville. Pick up Route 36 South and follow signs to Stony Brook State Park.

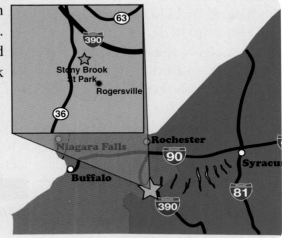

CONTACT...

Hours: Park is open all year. Gorge trails close Friday before Thanksgiving. Camping May - mid October. Pools open last weekend in June.
Call: (585) 335-8111, camping reservations 1-800-456-2267
Visit: www.nysparks.state.ny.us

Thirty Mile Point Lighthouse
BARKER, NY

Thirty Mile Point Lighthouse earns its name by being thirty miles east of the mouth of the Niagara River in Niagara County, N.Y. Built in 1875, the 70 foot tall structure can be found in Golden Hill State Park in Barker, New York, easily accessible from Route 18, the Seaway Trail.

A fantastic spiral staircase takes you to the top of the tower where, on a clear day, you can see Canada. Thirty Mile Point was selected by the Postal Service as one of five chosen in 1995 for its 'Lighthouses of the Great Lakes' stamp series.

How about spending the night in a lighthouse? You can! Thirty-Mile Point Lighthouse is one of the few that make this possible. The Lighthouse Suite has a kitchen with refrigerator, electric stove, microwave, cooking utensils, silverware and dishes. There is a very homey living room and a full bath. The 3 bedrooms all have queen size beds. You also have a private picnic area with a barbeque grill and picnic table right on the shoreline of Lake Ontario. Bring your own linens and towels.

Surrounding the lighthouse is a fifty-campsite park including trails, a playground, picnic area and a boat launch.

"How about spending the night in a lighthouse?"

Travel Tip...

Take advantage of all the apple farms and fruit and vegetable stands you'll be passing on your way to the lighthouse!

>> **ADMISSION:** Adults $1.00, Children $.50.

GETTIN' THERE...

Head West along the Lake Ontario State Parkway to its end. Continue West on Route 18 (Seaway Trail) and into Niagara County. Take a right onto Rt. 269 and a left onto Lower Lake Road. Look for signs to Golden Hill State Park.

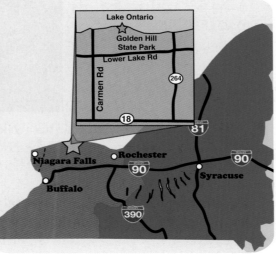

CONTACT...

Hours: Camping season begins in mid-April and ends in mid-October. The Lighthouse is open to tours daily 10am-6pm from July 4th to Labor Day. Overnight at the lighthouse is available year round.
Call: 1-800 456-2267 or **Visit:** www.nysparks.state.ny.us

Whirlpool Jet Boats
LEWISTON, NY

"Don't want to get your hair wet? 'Jet Dome' trips are available as well!" »

How about a boat ride? This one is a thrill a minute. All 45 minutes! That's how long you'll be taking on class 5 rapids, turning 360's and enjoying the beauty of nature all along the mighty Niagara River.

Whirlpool Jet Boat rides begin at the South Water Street Landing in Lewiston, New York every day May through October. They are in their 15th year of taking people of all ages (6 years old minimum) on an exhilarating jet boat ride into the Niagara River Gorge including the Niagara Whirlpool and the Devil's Hole Rapids.

You DO get very WET!!!! A wall of water will hit you no matter where you sit on the 1500 horsepower boat. That's why 'wet gear' is a must. Be wise and bring a change of clothes for this outdoor adventure. You'll want to be wearing either a bathing suit or shorts underneath the supplied 'wool sweater', 'yellow poncho' and 'life vest'.

"A wall of water will hit you no matter where you sit on the 1500 horsepower boat!"

Travel Tip...

You can save money by reserving your tickets online at **www.whirlpooljet.com**!

ADMISSION: Wet Jet $56 Adults, $47 (6-13). Discounts for groups of 10 or more. You must be in good health, at least 44 inches tall and at least 6 years old. You will fill out and sign a waiver form. Reservations are strongly recommended by calling or online. Jet Dome rides (covered boat) have different requirements.

GETTIN' THERE...

NYS Thruway to I-290 West. Take I-190 North toward Niagara Falls. From there, exit onto Rt. 265, exit #25A toward Lewiston. Turn left onto NY-265, Military Road, then a right onto Lewiston Rd. / NY-104. Take the Rt-104 West / Rt-18F N Ramp. Turn 'slight right' onto NY-104 / NY-18F Center Street. Now you are in Lewiston! Follow Center St. all the way to the end.

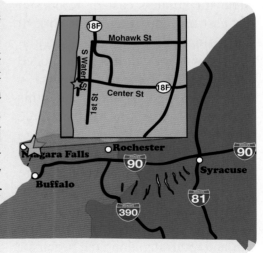

CONTACT...

Hours: Boat trip times from 10am to 5:30pm. (7pm during July and August)

Call: (888) 438-4444 or **Visit:** www.whirlpooljet.com

Chimney Bluffs
WOLCOTT, NY

What is Chimney Bluffs? That seems to be the big question. It may be closer than you think yet it looks like something from far, far away! Chimney Bluffs is actually a state park about 40 minutes east of Rochester just east of Sodus Bay, New York. It is a geological formation called a glacial moraine, which has been eroded into a series of knife-edge fingers.

Find a good day and this 'Getaway' can be fun for the whole family, especially if you like to go on hikes. Sneakers work well as do typical hiking shoes or boots. There are many choices for a hike at Chimney Bluffs. The full hike takes you along the cliff top for the first half and returning along the beach, or you can follow the beach and return to the path along the top of the hill. In either case, be sure to be very careful along the top of the hill overlooking the bluffs.

Many do not realize that the edge of the cliffs have very little support underneath and could give-way. Do not stand close to the edge. There are many warning signs all along the way. Day-use services include picnic areas, nature trails and restrooms. Household pets only, caged or on a leash.

You'll be surprised at how many people have never heard of Chimney Bluffs. Most who know about it would rather it be a secret. Well, the secret is out, but never fear. There's enough Chimney Bluffs for everyone. Enjoy!

"Most who know about it would rather it be a secret."

Travel Tip...

Try to go late in the day to catch the sunset. It is then that the 'chimnies' are really great to see at the top of the bluffs. By the way, the shore is rocky but swimming in the summer is possible. »

» **ADMISSION:** NONE! just be careful!

GETTIN' THERE...

From Route 104 near Sodus, NY, get onto Route 14 North. This will take you to the town of Alton. Turn right onto Old Ridge Rd. Go left onto Lake Bluff Rd. then a right onto Lummis-ville Rd. Look for a left on East Bay Rd. and follow it down to the lake. You'll note that East Bay Rd. begins to bear right to go along the lake shore. Go straight ahead instead and look for the parking lot.

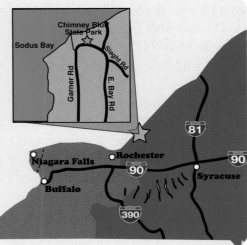

CONTACT...

Hours: Open year round, dawn to dusk.
Call: (315) 947-5205 or **Visit:** www.nysparks.state.ny.us

Cooperstown

COOPERSTOWN, NY

Cooperstown is more than Baseball! It may be hard to believe because everywhere you go...baseball! But if you look closer as you stroll this very walkable village, you'll see antiques and art... B&B's and boat rides. Add a burst of color if you visit in the fall and this getaway is perfect for the whole family!

I will admit, the biggest draw in Cooperstown is The National Baseball Hall of Fame. The busiest and most crowded time of year here is the Hall of Fame Weekend in August and held at the birthplace of baseball, Doubleday Field. This is a very popular weekend so plan well in advance.

There is plenty of metered parking on Main Street. You may also want to use the big parking lot in front of Doubleday Field.

If you're spending the night in Cooperstown, you have a choice of many bed & breakfasts, beautiful inns and a few basic motels. The Otesaga Hotel is the biggest and most luxurious accommodation. It sits majestically on Otsego Lake.

Something other than baseball? The Farmers' Museum is where rural American life comes alive each season with a re-creation of an American village on the land that has been part of a working farm since the 1790's. The heart of this attraction is the 1845 village with more than 20 buildings relocated from small towns across central New York. There is a museum shop and general store.

The Fenimore Art Museum has a wonderful collection of American fine art, folk art and North American indian art. The eleven galleries in the mansion can be found right across the street from The Farmers' Museum.

"Cooperstown is more than baseball!"

ATTRACTION...

If you're into baseball memorabilia and baseball souvenirs, its here! Also, finding something to eat is pretty easy because you have so many choices. My favorite is where the locals hangout, The Cooperstown Diner, a little place right on Main Street almost across from Doubleday Field. Order the burger. It's huge!

ADMISSION: Baseball Hall of Fame: Adults $16.50, Seniors $11, Ages (7-12) $6, Under 7 free! Military free, AAA discounts. **Farmers' Museum:** Adults $9 to $11 ages (7-12) $4 to $5, depending on the time of year. Under 7 are free. **Fenimore Art Museum:** Adults $11, Seniors $9.50, Children (7-12) $5, 6 and under are free.

GETTIN' THERE...

From the West, New York State Thruway to exit #30 (Herkimer). Head South on Rt. 28 and follow the signs to Cooperstown. From the East, NYS Thruway to exit #29 (Canajoharie) then Rts. 10, 20 & 80.

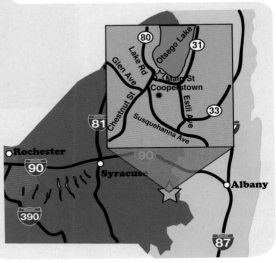

CONTACT...

Hours: Baseball Hall of Fame: Daily, 9 a.m. to 5 p.m. (off season)
From the day after Labor Day through Thursday before Memorial Day Weekend. Summer Hours: Daily, 9 a.m. to 9 p.m. From Friday of Memorial Day Weekend through Labor Day Monday.
Farmer's Museum: April - October **Fenimore Art Museum:** April - December.
Call: 1-888-425-5633 or **Visit:** www.baseballhalloffame.org
Call: (607) 547-1450 or **Visit:** www.farmersmuseum.org
Call: (607) 547-1400 or **Visit:** www.fenimoreartmuseum.org

Corning Museum of Glass
CORNING, NY

"The perfect place to perk up your day"

The cafe is stocked with pizzas, hot entrees, soup and salads. Open 11am-5pm daily.

Jump in the car with the whole family this weekend and head into the southern tier for a great day-trip. You'll find a gem of a museum in the Crystal City, Corning, New York.

Explore 3,500 years of glass making in the endless maze of galleries at the Corning Museum of Glass.

This getaway is a big hit with kids because of fun activities like hands-on science and glass making demos. You can even make your own glass! The Museum Glass Store and two restaurants to choose from make for a complete experience. Plan on spending from 3 to 4 hours touring the museum.

A short walk from the Museum of Glass over the pedestrian bridge will take you to historic Market Street. This is where you will find many other restaurant choices, from hot dogs to high-end. The shopping is also pretty extensive with stores covering a 4-block area. And there's even the new Palace Theatre in the middle of town for current run movies!

"This getaway is a big hit with kids."

TRAVEL TIP...

In addition to free parking at the museum, there is free shuttle service to the Rockwell Museum and to historic Market Street! Combine your trip with the Rockwell Museum and save money! Also, the museum participates in a number of hotel weekend packages.

>> **ADMISSION:** Adults $12.50, Children under age 17 FREE! Students and (55+) $11.25. AAA discounts.

GETTIN' THERE...

I-390 South to I-86 East (NY-17E) In Corning, get off at exit #46. Turn right at the end of the ramp. Look for the Visitor's Center immediately on your right. The free shuttle bus will take you to the museum!

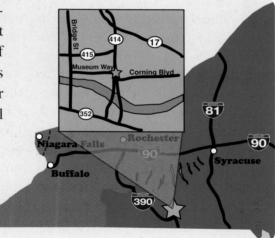

CONTACT...

Hours: Open year round 9am - 5pm (summers hours 9am - 8pm).
Tip: Check out the wine country link for hotel weekend packages.
www.fingerlakeswinecountry.com
Call: 1-800-732-6845 or **Visit:** www.cmog.org

Enchanted Forest
OLD FORGE, NY

There's a giant roaming the forest in Old Forge! He's been greeting visitors to Enchanted Forest since 1956. Standing 19 feet tall, Paul Bunyan continues to be a sort of mascot to this great Adirondack park that has always been known for Storybook Land. Kids today still enjoy the fairytale characters that live along the shaded, wooded trail. It leads to a petting zoo where kids can feed the animals.

Thankfully, Enchanted Forest hasn't changed a lot since we were kids. They have managed to hold on to the past while adding something new. Water Safari! High-speed water slides, kiddie slides and a Lazy River make this addition perfect for hot summer days in Old Forge, NY.

Planning to spend the night? Old Forge has many accommodation choices with everything from hotels, motels, lodges and campgrounds.

How about a typical Adirondack motel? I found a good one, just like the kind we went to as kids. "19th Green Motel", Route 28, has 13 clean and affordable units with an outdoor pool. Request room # 1, a big room on the end of the building. Be sure to look for 'Chance', the motel dog! (315) 369-3575

"Perfect for hot summer days!"

Travel Tip...

Arrive at Enchanted Forest after 3pm and the next day is free! Expect lighter crowds on Mondays and Fridays!

ADMISSION: One price includes both parks. Ages (3-11) $22.95, (12 and over) $25.95, 2 and under are free. (all prices plus tax) **Free Parking!**

GETTIN' THERE...

From NYS Thruway exit # 31 (Utica) head North on Rt. 12. Pick up Rt. 28 North to Old Forge. Travel time, about 1 hour from Utica, N.Y.

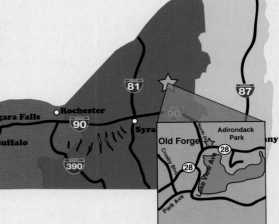

CONTACT...

Hours: Open 7 days a week Mid-June through Labor Day. Opening Week 10am-4pm, 2nd week and mid August through Labor Day 9:30am-6pm, Mid-June through mid-August 9:30am-7pm.
Call: (315) 369-6145 or **Visit:** www.watersafari.com

Esperanza Mansion
BLUFF POINT, NY

I had heard that there was an old mansion on 'the bluff' overlooking Keuka Lake built in the 1800's that had been renovated and was quite the 'talk of the town'. I decided to take a road-trip to check it out.

What a wonderful addition to the beauty of the Finger Lakes! The Esperanza Mansion is a Greek Revival style structure that was built by John Nicholas Rose in 1838. The renovated mansion, now an elegant resort, is a National Historic Landmark.

The nine lavish guest bedrooms nestled within the mansion are named for varieties of grapes grown in the Finger Lakes region. The mansion offers seven premium over-sized rooms, and two deluxe rooms. The Pinot Noir and the Chardonnay have a connecting door that may be opened to form a two-room suite.

Those who are looking for that special feeling that comes from staying in a historic landmark building with modern amenities will enjoy private bathrooms, individual in-room heat and air condition control, flat-screen cable TV, internet access, canopy and sleigh beds, period decor, and decorative fireplaces. A bottle of Finger Lakes wine and continental breakfast are complimentary with your stay.

For a bit less money, you can choose a room at " Inn at Esperanza", right next door to the mansion. 21 drive-up cottage-style rooms that are a bit less formal.

Dining at Esperanza is available for lunch and dinner Tuesdays through Saturdays. They do weddings and banquets for large and small groups. State of the art facilities respectfully surrounded by the grace and charm of the mansion.

"What a wonderful addition to the beauty of the Finger Lakes!"

Travel Tip...

Dress casual is the way to go. No "tie" necessary, unless you want to. You will see all styles of dress. All are welcome!

Ask about lunch and a tour of Keuka Lake aboard The Esperanza Rose! (see page 96)

> **ADMISSION:** Mansion and Inn rates start at $185 a night. Seasonal rates available.

GETTIN THERE...

From NYS Thruway exit #42 take Route 14 South through Geneva, N.Y. to the intersection with Route 54 West (about 20 miles from the Thruway). Take Route 54 West 4 miles to Penn Yan. Turn left on Main, right on Elm, and straight through onto Route 54A. The Esperanza Mansion will be on your right, approximately 7 miles outside of Penn Yan.

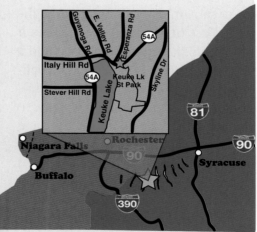

CONTACT...

Hours: Year round (closed January).
Call: 1-866-927-4400 or **Visit:** www.esperanzamansion.com

Farm Sanctuary
WATKINS GLEN, NY

If you love cows, horses, chickens and pigs, this very affordable getaway is for you! Animals at The Farm Sanctuary in Schuyler County have found a safe place on this 175-acre New York farm set amidst rolling green hills just West of Watkins Glen. It is a 45-minute drive west of Ithaca and a 90-minute drive southeast of Rochester. This getaway is a national, non-profit organization dedicated to changing the way society views and treats farm animals. Many of the animals you'll meet have been rescued from abusive conditions and cruel practices.

Your tour begins at "The People Barn" where you will experience a unique visitor center filled with displays, literature and videos. Kids will enjoy the "Kids Korner" area! Also note the 'Wall of Fame' with autographed photos of the 'big names'

that support the cause. You might even find yourself adopting and sponsoring one of the animals to help support the farm's operation.

I was amazed at the size of the cows and pigs! You know they've been treated well here because they are huge! This getaway is a great opportunity for the kids who have never been on a farm. The farm even has B&B cabins available! (reserve at (607) 583-2225 ext. 230)

Mike spends time with the cows!

"Adoption and sponsorship of animals helps to support the farm's operation."

Travel Tip...

Proper attire is key to making the most of this getaway. Wear clothes that you don't mind getting dirty and be sure to bring a pair of boots so you don't ruin your new sneakers!

ADMISSION: Adults $2.00, Children (under 12) $1.00.

GETTIN' THERE...

NYS Thruway exit #42 (Geneva) to Route 14 South along Seneca Lake to Watkins Glen. In town, pick up Route 409 West then a right turn onto Route 23/28. Stay on Route 23 as it branches off to the left. Continue on Route 23 for 8 miles then a left onto Aikens Road. Go 2 miles to the Visitor Center.

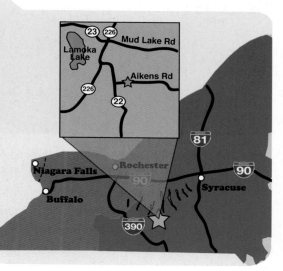

CONTACT...

Hours: Wednesday - Sunday. Hourly tours begin at 11am with the last tour at 3pm.

Call: (607) 583- 2225 or **Visit:** www.farmsanctuary.org

Harris Hill Soaring

ELMIRA, NY

> **"What a wonderful view from 2000 feet in the air!"**
> The ride lasts 15 to 20 minutes, depending on the weather.

No motor! Just you and the air! Catching a ride aboard a 'glider' may be one of the best ways to see the colors of Fall. You'll find yourself hundreds of feet above the hills over Elmira, New York when you head to Harris Hill Soaring Center, Route 352 in Chemung County.

A weekend afternoon here any time in the spring, summer or fall can make for a great getaway for a once-in-a-lifetime thrill. Your very own pilot, seated behind you, will fly the glider from take off to landing. A tow plane with an engine takes you down the runway and eventually sets you free from the cable attached to the glider. Surrounded by only a clear bubble in the front of the glider, you'll be able to see for miles. Exhilerating!

Harris Hill's history is long and represented very well in the National Soaring Museum. A must-see!

"No Motor! Just you and the air!"

While you're in the area, head to the Chemung County Airport to visit The Wings of Eagles Discovery Center to see one of the best 'warbird aircraft' collections in the world including the B-26 and Spitfire.

> **ADMISSION:** Glider Rides $65-$75.

GETTIN' THERE...

I-390 South becomes I-86 in the southern tier. Just past Corning, N.Y. take exit #48 to Route 352. Head South and look for signs to the 'Soaring Center'. Be careful, the signs are small! One of the signs will indicate a left turn. Take it and go up the hill until you see a huge white 'wing' standing on end. Take a right turn.

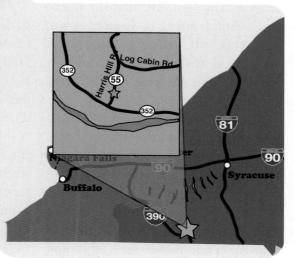

CONTACT...

Hours: April-October, No reservations, first come, first served. Weekends only early April, Full 7-Days a week beginning late June. Weather permitting.

Call: (607) 734-0641 or **Visit:** www.harrishillsoaring.org

Inn at Cooperstown
COOPERSTOWN, NY

This inn has made the list! The Inn at Cooperstown can be found in the Distinguished Inns of North America publication. You will also find the inn at 16 Chestnut Street in Cooperstown, New York. If you're looking for a cozy B&B with perfect location in one of America's great small towns, this is it!

Built in 1874 as the annex to the posh Hotel Fenimore, the inn was fully restored in 1985 and today accommodates travelers from all around. There are 17 guest rooms, all with private bath and air conditioning. Some can accommodate families and there are adjoining rooms for larger parties. There is also a suite with sitting room, wet bar and refrigerator. One amenity that brings a touch of the present to the past is a CD player in each room. Phones and TVs can be found in the com-

mon rooms downstairs. Continental breakfast is included with your room rate and served in the first floor dining room.

The Inn at Cooperstown is perfectly situated. Getting to the town's attractions, like the Baseball Hall of Fame, is only a short walk away. Guest parking is right behind the inn. Pets cannot be accommodated.

Also, while you're in Cooperstown, travel up the road to two other big attractions filled with great local history. The Farmers' Museum and the James Fenimore Art Museum.

"The Inn at Cooperstown is perfectly situated."

Travel Tip...

Summer months can be very busy in Cooperstown so book rooms early for June, July and August. Ask for a 'premium room' facing the front. Furnishings and beds have an extra nice touch.

ADMISSION: Rooms range from $102 to $330 per night.

GETTIN' THERE...

NYS Thruway to exit #30 (Herkimer). Follow Route 28 South to Cooperstown. After entering the village, turn left onto Chestnut St. and go through the traffic light. The 'Inn' is the third building on your left.

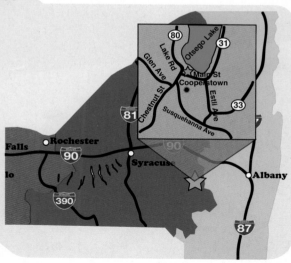

CONTACT...

Call: (607) 547-5756 or **Visit:** www.innatcooperstown.com

Welcome to Lake Country

Treleaven
KING FERRY
WINERY

The Finger Lakes region holds surprises around every corner and along winding wine trails that canvas the beautiful landscape. Being this close to an area that is so spectacular is truly special. Let's explore three of the Finger Lakes and all that they hold for great day trips and weekends away!

Lake Country
CAYUGA LAKE, NY

Cayuga Lake's west side is filled with fantastic wineries along the wine trail, Rt. 89. But for a real unexpected treat, along come owners and vintners that are bringing a lot of surprises to Cayuga's East side. A winding State Route 90 takes you through small towns and villages like Cayuga, Union Springs and Aurora. Just before you go through the town of Aurora, N.Y., you may want to spend a bit of time at the famous tableware and furnishings manufacturer MacKenzie-Childs. If you plan to spend the night nearby, I recommend The Aurora Inn.

There may be only two wineries on this side of the lake, but they are two of the best! Finger Lakes wines have come a long way and you'll agree after enjoying a 'tasting' at 'Long Point Winery'. Here, they specialize in dry reds that are barrel-aged 18-33 months. There is a lot of love put into these award-winning wines! White wines include Rieslings, Chardonnay and Sauvignion Blanc. Expect very laid-back surroundings with spectacular views of Cayuga Lake! Open April-December daily 10am-5:30pm and February-March Fri-Sunday 12pm-5pm. (315) 364-6990

You're not far from Cayuga Lake's other eastside winery 'King Ferry Winery' with daily tastings of reds and whites. Their award-winning Chardonnays are incredible! Look for signs off of State Rt. 90.

Long Point Winery's barrel-aged wine.

> *"There may only be two wineries on this side of the lake, but they are two of the best!"*

ATTRACTION...

Just south of Aurora, look for Pumpkin Hill, a cozy old farmhouse surrounded by gardens. You'll discover delicious and imaginative food served either inside or out. Go for Cookie's Chicken Pot Pie! Mmmmm!

ADMISSION: Wine tastings at minimal cost!

GETTIN' THERE...

From NYS Thruway exit #41, turn right then left onto Route 318. Continue East for approximately 6 miles and then a right turn onto State Route 90 to Cayuga Lakes East side.

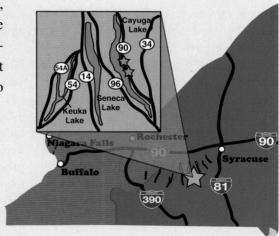

CONTACT...

Call: (315) 364-6990 for Long Point Winery and (315) 364-5100 for King Ferry Winery.
Visit: www.longpointwinery.com or www.treleavenwines.com

Lake Country
KEUKA LAKE, NY

alled the 'Lady of the Lakes' because of its natural beauty, Keuka Lake offers so many getaway opportunities. While both sides of the lake have wineries, there is a greater concentration on Keuka's west side. A good starting point is from Hammondsport on Keuka Lake's southern tip. This is what a Finger Lakes village is supposed to look like! Quaint stores and antique shops, restaurants and a beautiful bright, white church next to the village park, complete with gazebo.

Further along County Rt. 76 on your left side, sitting majestically on the hill, you'll see Heron Hills. From the vaulted ceiling tasting room to the extensive gift shop and Blue Heron Café , you can easily spend a few hours here. This is one of the few wineries offering an outdoor terrace for lunch and dinner with a wonderful view of Keuka Lake.

Continuing north on County Rt. 76, slow down so you won't miss the occasional pottery maker or roadside fun at Wild Goose Chase Antiques, adding to the color and character of this Finger Lakes wine trail.

Be sure to follow the signs to Dr. Konstantin Frank's winery. This may be the most popular winery in the region, known for award-winning dry Riesling and Finger Lakes Champagne.

Further on up the road near Branchport, stop by a winery that takes you on a tour! Hunt Country Vineyards has been in the family for 6 generations, a farm that grows the grapes, works the land and produces very good wines. They first achieved a national reputation as a premier producer of 'ice wine'. Be sure to see the entire wine making process on their guided tours for only $2.50. This is what makes Hunt Country Vineyards different from most of the others! Look for 'Gus', the dog! He greets everyone! Back onto Rt. 54A to Penn Yan and onto Rt. 54 south for Keuka Lake's new east side winery, Rooster Hill Vineyards. Bring a picnic and enjoy a classic Finger Lakes view on their stone patio.

"Called the 'Lady of the Lakes' because of its natural beauty!"

ATTRACTION...

On your way to Keuka's East side, you may want to explore the hidden gem amongst the trees on the banks of Bluff Point, Garrett Chapel. Enter the State Park entrance off of 54A and look for Skyline Drive.

ADMISSION: Wine tastings range from one to five dollars.

GETTIN THERE...

NYS Thruway to exit #42 (Geneva) and South on Route 14. Continue South on Route 14 all along Seneca Lake and pick up Route 54 West in Dresden into Penn Yan. In Penn Yan, follow Route 54A into Branchport then continue South along Keuka Lake's West side into Hammondsport. Or, continue South on Route 54 in Penn Yan along Keuka Lake's East side.

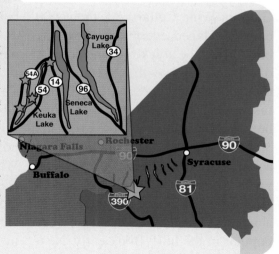

CONTACT...

Hours: Garrett Chapel March- November. **Hunt Country** open year round. **Dr. Konstantin Frank's Winery** open year round. **Heron Hill** open year round.

Call: 1-800-946-3289 or **Visit:** www.huntwines.com
Call: (315) 536-4773 or **Visit:** www.garrettchapel.org
Call: 1-800-441-4241 or **Visit:** www.heronhill.com
Call: 1-800-320-0735 or **Visit:** www.drfrankwines.com

Lake Country
SENECA LAKE, NY

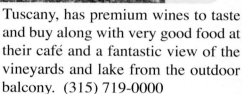

Head east over the hills from Keuka Lake to Rt.14 on Seneca Lake and discover one of the most popular of the 36 wineries, Glenora Wine Cellars. At about 600 cases produced every day, they stay busy. You'll be able to see the process of wine making with a guided wine tour followed by the traditional wine tasting. The one big difference between Glenora and all the rest is the 30-room inn! The upscale and cozy accommodations all have breathtaking views of the vineyards and Seneca Lake from either a top floor balcony or a 1st floor deck. Weekends are very popular in the fall! Book early. Next to the Inn is Veraison's Restaurant, which has both indoor and outdoor seating for lunch and dinner.

On the sometimes overlooked 'east side' of Seneca Lake, just south of Geneva on Route 96A, you'll make some great discoveries. Ventosa Vineyards, with a touch of Tuscany, has premium wines to taste and buy along with very good food at their café and a fantastic view of the vineyards and lake from the outdoor balcony. (315) 719-0000

From Rt. 96A, a quick right turn onto East Lake Road will take you on a more scenic route, and to Lerch Road. This is where you'll find 4 wineries all together for your enjoyment. The original Nagy's New Land Estate has now been joined by Stony Lonesome Wine Cellars, Passion Feet Vineyards & Wine Barn and the edgy Rogue's Hollow. From dry to sweet, the wines are designed to please everyone, no matter what your taste. Caution: The humor at Rogue's Hollow could be taken, as they say 'in pour taste'. This Louisiana bayou-like building, complete with pond, is the one people talk about most. Unlike the other three, wine tasting here is done out of a shot glass! Very casual and fun!

"You'll make some great discoveries!"

Travel Tip...

You are only 8 miles north of the Watkins Glen Gorge. This is a fantastic family adventure especially on a hot summer day!

Attraction...

There's a castle on the lake! Just South of Geneva, NY on Route 14, find beautiful Belhurst Castle on the shores of Seneca Lake. A good stop on the Seneca Wine Trail to dine, spend the night or just to visit this historic attraction.

ADMISSION: Wine tastings range from one to five dollars.

Gettin' There...

Take NYS Thruway exit #42 (Geneva) and South on Route 14. This will take you along Seneca Lake's West side to access many wineries including Glenora Wine Cellars and into Watkins Glen. Or East on Routes 5 & 20 in Geneva to Route 96A South along Seneca Lake's East side to access wineries like Three Brothers.

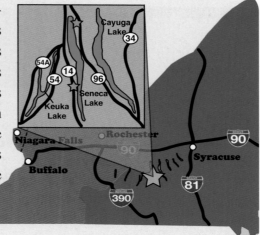

Contact...

Hours: Glenora Wine Cellars, Three Brothers Wineries & Estates, Ventosa Vineyards open year-round.
Call: 1-800-243-5513 or **Visit:** www.glenora.com
Call: (315) 585-4432 or **Visit:** www.3brotherswinery.com
Call: (315) 719-0000 or **Visit:** www.ventosavineyards.com

MacKenzie-Childs

AURORA, NY

"MacKenzie - Childs hand painted ceramics and furniture are popular world wide!"

A day-trip to MacKenzie-Childs provides you with an enjoyable road-trip along state route 90 on the eastern shores of Cayuga Lake and onto an amazing compound of creativity and wonder. Enter along a winding brick driveway to 65 acres of gardens, ponds and total tranquility. The whole family can enjoy this Finger Lakes Getaway!

MacKenzie-Childs is the world-renowned maker of hand-painted majolica tableware and home furnishings. You can watch a Studio Tour video in the Visitor Center that takes you behind the scenes from design through production with talented artisans at work. Live demonstrations are also offered daily.

There's a wonderful gift shop offering the complete line of MacKenzie-Childs products and gifts from around the world.

By the way, you are only minutes away from the historic village of Aurora for lunch or dinner!

"An amazing compound of creativity and wonder!"

ATTRACTION...

Tour an exquisitely restored Victorian farmhouse, open to the public. Daily guided tours are free and take you through 15 rooms on 3 floors. Check ahead for tour times. They change seasonally.

ADMISSION: FREE!

GETTIN' THERE...

NYS Thruway to Waterloo exit #41. Head East on Route 318 to State Route 90. Travel South 14 miles to find MacKenzie-Childs on your left side, just one mile before the town of Aurora, New York.

CONTACT...

Hours: Open all year. Grounds open daily from 9:30am to 6:30pm.
Call: (315) 364-7123 or (888) 665-1999
Visit: **www.mackenzie-childs.com**

Museum of the Earth

ITHACA, NY

"Cecil the Coelophysis welcomes you!" ∧

There's been a major discovery in Ithaca, New York! People are discovering the history of the earth. The Museum of the Earth has been here since 2003 but a lot of people have yet to visit the 18,000 square feet of earthly specimens. This is a popular family getaway because there is something here for everyone.

The big attraction is the Hyde Park Mastodon. Found in someone's back yard, it is one of the most complete skeletons ever unearthed! The 40 foot Right Whale skeleton suspended in the lobby is also a big favorite. You will be able to touch and feel history through hands-on exploration of fossils at the Discovery Stations Fossil Lab, Dino Lab and Ice Lab.

Housing 1000's of specimens, this is one of the largest collections in the United States and it's right here near Ithaca, New York. Expect to spend about 2-hours to explore. When you arrive, look for the museum's dinosaur mascot Cecil!

"The Mastodon is one of the most complete skeletons ever unearthed!"

ADMISSION: $8 Adults, $5 Seniors/Students, $3 ages 4-17, free 3 and under.

GETTIN' THERE...

NYS Thruway exit #42 to Route 14 toward Geneva/Lyons. Turn right onto Route 14 South. Merge onto route 96A South to route 96 South for about 40 miles. The Museum of the Earth is on your left after you pass the Cayuga Medical Center.

CONTACT...

Hours: Year round, Summer Hours Monday-Saturday 10am-5pm, Sunday 11am-5pm. Winter Hours: Monday and Wednesday through Saturday 10AM to 5PM. Sunday 11AM-5PM. Closed Tuesdays.

Call: (607) 273-6623 Ext. 33 or **Visit:** www.museumoftheearth.org

Red Mill Inn
BALDWINSVILLE, NY

"All thirty-two rooms have a river or canal view!"

ON THE ERIE CANAL AT LOCK 24
The Red Mill Inn
Est. 2006
BALDWINSVILLE, NY

Take one very old grist mill from the early 1800's and convert it to a very comfortable 32-room hotel, and you've just described The Red Mill Inn in Baldwinsville, New York. A great deal of attention and money has gone into this endeavor sitting on Paper Mill Island between the Seneca River and the Erie Canal.

Locals and out-of-towners make the inn a regular overnight destination. The moment you walk in, you'll see why it is so popular. Their warm staff will greet you before you make your way to a very welcoming guest room.

Each room is different. It would be hard to find any two alike. The only thing most of them have in common is the original wooden beams that are still in place from the original grist mill structure. On your visit, note the great attention to detail and quality. Every room features Stickley furniture!

There are some very impressive suites at The Red Mill Inn complete with an excellent river view. The absence of a restaurant and bar on the property is not a mistake. The owners decided to enhance the area businesses and not compete with them.

"The moment you walk in, you'll see why it's so popular!"

Travel Tip...

If you like small, warm and cozy, try a 'loft room' up on the 3rd floor! And don't forget your fishing pole! Guests at the inn have access to private fishing on the banks of the Seneca River!

ADMISSION: From $109 to $299. (ask about any special rates)

GETTIN' THERE...

Exit #39 from the NYS Thruway to Rt. I-690 North. Take the Van Buren exit and a right turn onto Van Buren Road. Follow to the traffic light and a left onto Route 48. You will see the inn just after your 2nd traffic light, just before the bridge over the river.

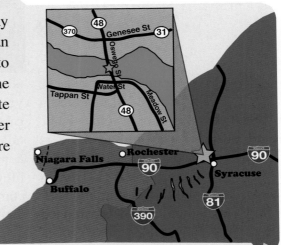

CONTACT...

Hours: Open year round.
Call: 1-800-841-0411 or (315) 635-4871
Visit: www.theredmillinn.com

Robert H. Treman State Park

ITHACA, NY

"Enjoy nine miles of hiking trails and swimming beneath a waterfall!"

C ount them! There are 12 waterfalls in all, including the 115-foot Lucifer Falls. Find all of these natural wonders along a mile-and-a-half wooded trail in the very scenic Robert H. Treman State Park. Add to this nine miles of hiking trails and an old-fashioned swimming hole and you've got a great family day-trip getaway.

Getting there is half the fun when you travel the western shore of Cayuga Lake along Route 89 in the Finger Lakes.

Your first turn into the park takes you to the Lower Park. Park admission is $7 per car. This is where you'll find RV sites, tent camping, cabins, picnicking and the ol' swimmin' hole! The stream-fed pool beneath a waterfall has a diving board and lifeguard on duty along with very comfortable and clean locker room facilities.

If you're looking for a more peaceful and quiet section of the park, head to the Upper Park entrance from Rt. 327. This is also the most beautiful part of the gorge and where you'll have the most picture-taking opportunities.

"There are twelve waterfalls in all, including the 115-foot Lucifer Falls!"

Travel Tip...

Use your park admission to get into all other state parks in the area on the same day, like Buttermilk Falls, Taughannock Falls and Watkins Glen State Park. Also, pets must be caged or leashed with certificate of proof of rabies inoculation.

ADMISSION: $7.00 per car.

GETTIN' THERE...

NYS Thruway exit #41. Go East on Rt. 318 to 5&20, then South on Rt. 89. In Ithaca, look for Rt. 13 and follow South for about 5 miles, then a right turn onto Route 327. Look for park signs.

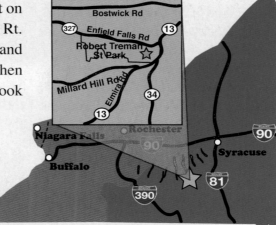

CONTACT...

Hours: Open all year. Gorge trails close early November. Camping mid-May through end of November.
Call: Park Office: (607) 273-3440
Camping Reservations: 1-800-456-2267
Visit: www.nysparks.state.ny.us

Rockwell Museum of Western Art
CORNING, NY

How about a getaway to one of the finest collections of Western art in the country? You'll find it in Corning, New York at The Rockwell Museum, 111 Cedar Street.

Three floors of breathtaking paintings and sculptures! See the work of Russell and Remington. Even one gallery devoted to the Western art of Andy Warhol. Call ahead to find out about the museum's impressive special exhibitions schedule.

This getaway is perfect for the whole family because the museum works hard to make this a great experience for kids too. Special art backpacks help lead children on an exciting journey through the West.

Don't worry about getting tired during your visit here. Simply head to the second floor to find the very comfortable Western lodge complete with couches and a fireplace. Prints, reproductions and books related to the museums collection and Western and Native American art can be found in the Museum Trading Post.

The Rockwell Museum of Western Art, a good reason to make the trip to the Southern Tier ...to see the best of the West!

"Three floors of breathtaking paintings and sculptures."

ADMISSION: Adults $6.50, Seniors (55+) and Students with ID $5.50, Ages 17 and under free!

GETTIN' THERE...

I-390 becomes I-86 into the southern tier. Take exit #46 in Corning, NY and follow signs to Rockwell Museum of Western Art. Parking available next to museum and on Market Street.

CONTACT...

Hours: Open year round, daily from 9am-5pm. Extended summer hours 9am-8pm. Closed: New Year's Day, Thanksgiving Day, Christmas Eve & Christmas Day
Call: (607) 937-5386 or **Visit:** www.rockwellmuseum.org

Rosamond Gifford Zoo
SYRACUSE, NY

Great in winter...it's mostly inside! It's tough to find a good family getaway when it's snowy and cold. How about heading to the zoo? Don't worry! This zoo is 60% inside! The Rosamond Gifford Zoo at Burnet Park in Syracuse, New York has a collection of more than 1000 animals.

It gets pretty tropical inside the zoo's huge ecosystem-themed open-air aviary. Keep your eyes open! There are more than 80 birds in here!

Other inside fun...fish, amphibians, reptiles, birds and mammals that take you on a journey through time in the USS Antiquities area. Then of course, there are the bats, sloths, lions, meerkats and monkeys.

Check out the Jungle Cafe if you get hungry and a very large and colorful gift shop.

Care to venture outside? Walk the 1/2-mile trail through the zoo's natural habitat and don't miss the 50,000 gallon freshwater Penquin Exhibit! The zoo's outside holds Reindeer, Bighorn Sheep, Grey Wolf, Domestic Yak, Bison, Snow Leopard, Bear and Asian Elephant.

Winter, spring, summer or fall, this getaway is perfect anytime of year!

"Great in winter...it's mostly inside!"

Travel Tip...

Leave Fido at home! Pets are NOT permitted on zoo grounds, but you CAN bring your appetite.

ADMISSION: Adults (16-61) \$6.50, Children (3-15) \$4, Students (16-21 w/ID) \$4.50, Seniors (62+) \$4.50, 2 and under are free. Group Rates. Free parking.

GETTIN' THERE...

1-90, NYS Thruway to exit #39. Get onto I-690 East to exit #8, Hiawatha Blvd. Turn right and follow road to end. At traffic light, go left on Erie Blvd. Turn right onto Geddes St., right on Seymour St., right onto Wilbur. The zoo is up on your left.

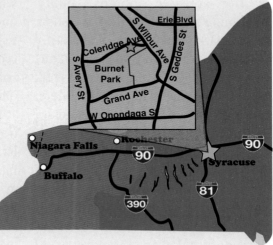

CONTACT...

Hours: Open every day 10am-4:30pm except Thanksgiving, Christmas and New Year's Day. Stroller rentals and free wheelchairs available. Handicap accessible.
Call: (315) 435-8511 or **Visit:** www.rosamondgiffordzoo.org

Skaneateles

SKANEATELES.NY

As pretty as a picture! The village of Skaneateles is truly one of the most beautiful small towns in the Finger Lakes region of upstate New York. In the summer months, public swimming is available from the shore of the park. Boat tours of beautiful Skaneateles Lake are also available. At just the right size, you can walk to most anything in the village. Meter parking is available on both sides of the street.

Shopping in town is one of the reasons many people make Skaneateles their destination choice. You'll find a great variety of shops and restaurants. Charles Dickens characters take to the streets of Skaneateles with *A Christmas Carol* theme on weekends beginning the Friday after Thanksgiving.

When it's time for lunch, I have a few favorites. If you want to grab a good deli sandwich and enjoy it in the park right on the lake, go across the street from the gazebo to the delicatessen. The food is good and fresh and easy to take-out. If you want to sit inside but still stay within budget, I recommend Doug's Fish Fry on Jordan Street. People come from all over to eat here and sometimes wait in line that can go out onto the sidewalk. Plan ahead!

Staying the night? Accommodations can be as simple as a motel on Rt. 20 as you come in to town, or an intimate stay in one of the many bed & breakfasts in the village, like The Sherwood Inn. (315) 685-3405

Whatever you decide, day-trip or overnight, the village of Skaneateles is as peaceful as can be. Weekdays aren't quite as busy as weekends in the summer, so plan accordingly. And Skaneateles in the Fall? ...Unbelievable!

"Truly one of the most beautiful small towns in the Finger Lakes region of upstate NY."

ATTRACTION...

Just outside of town on Route 20, look for Mirbeau Inn & Spa, a world class spa along with fine dining and romantic overnight accommodations.

Travel Tip...

If a bathroom stop is the first thing on the itinerary, go directly to the huge gazebo in the park along the lake. There are convenient restrooms below.

ADMISSION: FREE!

GETTIN' THERE...

Take NYS Thruway to the Weedsport exit #40. Travel South on Rt. 34, then a left (East) onto Rt. 20 in to Auburn. From there you're only a few minutes away from the village of Skaneateles.

CONTACT...

Call: (315) 685-0552 **Visit:** www.skaneateles.com
Call: (315) 685-1927 **Visit:** www.mirbeau.com
Call: (315) 685-3405 **Visit:** www.thesherwoodinn.com

Sodus Bay Lighthouse and Museum

SODUS POINT, NY

"Less than a mile from the lighthouse is the Sodus Outer Pierhead Light!" »

Travel along Lake Ontario's Seaway Trail between Rochester and Oswego and you'll encounter the beautiful "Old Lighthouse at Sodus Point". The first construction began in 1824, but after the Civil War, disrepair took over. The tower and keeper's residence were replaced in 1870. In fact, you can still see where the old tower once stood just in front of the new structure. The current tower still houses the original fresnel lens.

From the Sodus Bay Lighthouse, you can see another lighthouse at the end of the pier. This is where you'll find a 45-foot white pierhead light also known as the Sodus Outer Light. The light is now automated and still operational, guiding vessels into Sodus Bay with a glowing red lantern.

If you love lighthouses, this one is a beauty. You can climb the winding stairs to the top of the tower for a magnificent view!

The Lighthouse Museum features regional and maritime history. There is also a small gift shop, library, picnic sites and free parking. This getaway is 85% wheelchair accessible.

> ## *"If you love lighthouses, this one is a beauty."*

Travel Tip...

The Sodus Bay Historical Society holds several free outdoor concerts and events out on the lighthouse grounds from July 4th to September 2nd. Bring your lawn chair!

> **ADMISSION:** Adults $3, ages (11-17) $1, Under 11 free!

GETTIN' THERE...

From Rt. 104 in Wayne County, head North on Rt. 14 to the village of Sodus Point. Turn right onto Bay Street, then North onto Ontario St. and follow to the end. Look for signs to the lighthouse.

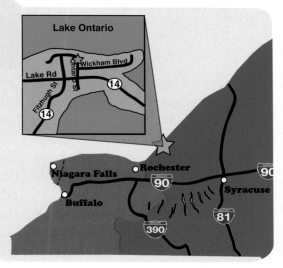

CONTACT...

Hours: May 1- October 31, 10am - 5pm Tuesday - Sunday. Closed Mondays except holidays.
Call: (315) 483-4936 or **Visit:** www.soduspointlighthouse.org

Sylvan Beach
SYLVAN BEACH, NY

"Take a break from the beach and cool off on a few rides!"

It's sooooo nice to go back in time to a place where life is still simple and fun. Welcome to Sylvan Beach on Oneida Lake in Oneida County. The beach, the amusement park, the cottages and campsites...it's all here!

When you arrive, the first thing you see is the old-time "Sylvan Beach Amusement Park". They haven't changed a thing after all these years. A fun-house, a roller coaster, Skee-ball and a Rochester connection, the Tilt-A-Whirl! It's the one from the old Olympic Park on Scottsville Road. Twenty-one rides in all with free admission! You only pay for the rides you want to ride on! Now that's 'yesterday'!

The beach is conveniently next to the amusement park, complete with lifeguards making it a safe place for families with kids. The water is pretty clean with sand and a few stones.

Sylvan beach has a number of restaurants in town including the town's most famous Eddie's Restaurant.

Pack the car and grab the family and take off for a summertime destination where you can show the kids how life used to be! Have fun!

"A summer time destination where you can show the kids how life used to be."

Travel Tip...

If you're looking to make it more than a day-trip, look for numerous campsites and cottages in the area.

ADMISSION: Beach admission free. Ride tickets available for purchase.

GETTIN' THERE...

Use the NYS Thruway to exit #34, the Canastota exit, then Rt. 13 North to Sylvan Beach. Out of Rochester, approximately a 2 hour drive.

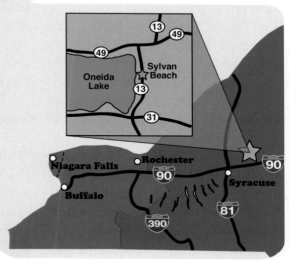

CONTACT...

Hours: Open April through September.
Visit: www.sylvanbeach.org

Taughannock Falls
TRUMANSBURG, NY

Taughannock Falls...higher than Niagara Falls? It's true, by about 21 feet...the highest waterfall in the Eastern U. S. Not far from Ithaca, Taughannock Falls State Park is in Trumansburgh, New York and is the perfect day-trip for outdoor enthusiasts. Gorge and rim trails offer spectacular views from above the falls and from below at the end of the gorge trail.

There is access from the Taughannock Falls State Park entrance parking lot along Route 89. ($7 fee) You can follow the 3/4 mile gorge trail along the waterway to the falls. Even on a hot summer day, the mostly shaded trail path is still comfortable. This trail is wide enough for baby carriages and wheelchairs alike. Also note that many people actually walk along the creek bed all the way to the falls.

Despite seeing people in the water near the falls, don't do it. Signs make it clear that one shouldn't go beyond the stone wall. As refreshing as it may look, the water is quite cold, very deep and dangerous. There is a swimming beach within the park on Cayuga Lake.

From Route 89, just north of the State Park entrance, there is a turn-off to a parking lot (free). Look for the "Falls Overlook" sign, which leads to an awesome view of the falls from a distance. You'll usually find artists set-up at this spot capturing the beauty on canvas.

"The highest waterfall in the Eastern U.S.!"

Travel Tip...

If you are a New York State resident 62 or older, on any weekday (except holidays), you can obtain free vehicle access to state parks and arboretums!

ADMISSION: Park admission $7.00. Pets: Household pets only, caged or on a leash not more than 6 feet. Proof of rabies inoculation. Not allowed in bathing areas.

GETTIN' THERE...

NYS Thruway to exit #41. Go South to Rt. 318 then East on 5 & 20. Jump on scenic Route 89 South all along beautiful Cayuga Lake, just 8 miles North of Ithaca, NY.

CONTACT...

Hours: Open year round. Camping season runs from the last weekend in March to mid-October. The rim trail closes in winter; the gorge trail remains open.

Call: 1-800-456-2267 or (607) 387-6739

Visit: www.nysparks.state.ny.us

The Esperanza Rose

BLUFF POINT, NY

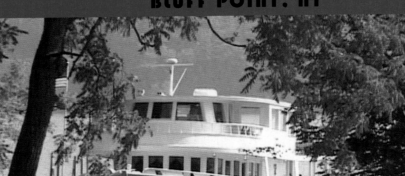

The Esperanza Rose sits majestically on Keuka Lake anticipating her next guests for another elegant cruise. This getaway puts you on-board a beautiful 65-foot vintage, wooden cruising vessel that has been sailing the waters of Keuka Lake since 2005. The ride is smooth and easy with so much to see and hear about, courtesy of the captain. Everything is done professionally on board the boat including great service! In the spring, summer and fall, lunch, dinner and sightseeing cruises are available from the docks at the northwest end of Keuka Lake in Branchport, New York.

Lunch and Dinner Cruises last 2 hours with your choice of an indoor, down-below, white tablecloth, setting, or my favorite, the more casual, up-on-deck, wind in your hair setting. Don't be afraid to bring the kids. They may get a chance to sit up front with the Captain of the Ship!

Special occasions and private events can be fun on The Esperanza Rose accommodating from 8 to 130 people!

This location in the Finger Lakes is only minutes away from Esperanza Mansion up on the hill, and the hidden-away Keuka Lake gem, Garrett Chapel on Bluff Point. When leaving The Esperanza Rose, continue south on scenic Route 54A to the quaint village of Hammondsport, only 17 miles away.

"The ride is smooth and easy with so much to see..."

Travel Tip...

Book in advance for October cruises on the Esperanza Rose. The incredible colors of fall all along the hills surrounding Keuka Lake are breathtaking... and very popular!

ADMISSION: Lunch cruise: Adult 29.95 Child 16.00. Sightseeing cruise: Adult 19.00 Child 14.00. Dinner cruise: Adult 43.95 Child 19.95. Taxes apply to food portion of cruise only.

GETTIN' THERE...

NYS Thruway (I-90) to exit #42. Follow Route 14 South through Geneva and continue along Seneca Lake. Look for Route 54 West and follow for 4 miles into Penn Yan. Pick up Route 54A West, travel 9 miles to the blinking light in Branchport. Turn left and look for the Esperanza Rose sign 1/4 mile up on your left.

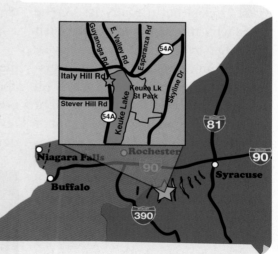

CONTACT...

Hours: Lunch cruises board at 11am, depart at 11:30am, return at 1:30pm. Dinner cruises board at 5pm, depart at 5:30pm, return at 7:30pm. Sightseeing Cruises last 1-1/2 hours with boarding at 2pm, departing at 2:30pm, returning at 4pm.

Call: 1-866-927-4400 or **Visit:** www.esperanzaboat.com

Watkins Glen State Park

WATKINS GLEN, NY

The gorge at Watkins Glen is....gorgeous! I couldn't resist but it really is. Maybe that's why thousands of people visit the gorge every year. Trails, caves, tunnels, whirlpools, waterfalls, a suspension bridge and much more on this incredible find at the south end of beautiful Seneca Lake. This is a lot of fun for the whole family but remember, there are 832 steps to get through the gorge, so bring good foot-gear and a bottle or two of water. The gorge is just one part of the 1000 acre Watkins Glen State Park.

Many people don't know it but Watkins Glen State Park is the most famous of all the Finger Lakes State Parks and is open year round. (The gorge is open the 1st week in May until Nov. 9th)

You'll find 305 fantastic camp-sites in a wooded area at the park and reservations can be made up to eleven months in advance by calling 1-800-456-2267.

The gorge isn't the only spot in the park that'll keep you cool. How about an Olympic-size swimming pool? They've got one at the upper level of the park open to campers and day-visitors.

"The most famous of all the Finger Lakes State Parks!"

Travel Tip...

If you happen to skip the refreshment stand near the park pool, you can always head into the village of Watkins Glen to find several restaurant choices. Small shops and antique stores abound!

ADMISSION: $7.00 per car.

GETTIN' THERE...

NYS Thruway to exit #42, Geneva, then South on Rt. 14 all along Seneca Lake into Watkins Glen. I would suggest following the road to the upper level of the park so that you can walk 'down' through the gorge. A shuttle bus will take you back up to the top.

CONTACT...

Hours: Park is open year round. Camping is available from early May to mid-October. Depending on the weather, the gorge trail is closed from early November to mid-May. Bow hunting for deer is permitted in season.

Call: (607) 535-4511, camping reservations 1-800-456-2267

Visit: www.nysparks.state.ny.us

Wellesley Island

THOUSAND ISLANDS, NY

Heading to The 1000 Islands this summer doesn't mean you have to battle big crowds. One of the best kept secrets that many tourists overlook is Wellesley Island!

Just after you cross the Thousand Islands Bridge, your first exit takes you to Wellesley Island. There's a great State Park here with cabins, camping grounds, hiking trails, beaches and a marina to rent a fishing boat. There's also a pretty nice golf course and country club on the island. Try the burger at Hackers. It's delicious!

Past the state park and heading west, the road starts to wind and narrow. You're about to go back in time as you enter the town of Thousand Island Park. Golf carts are the most used mode of transportation driven along unpaved roads past Victorian homes and cottages.

The Wellesley Hotel & Restaurant is the main attraction as you enter town. You'll find simple, old-time lodging and sensational dining courtesy of Chef Gerry Brinkman of Rochester, N.Y. He and his wife Diane have been running the hotel every season since 2003. No phone, no TV. The air-conditioning comes from the breezes off the St. Lawrence River. The hotel is the perfect place for families and couples looking to leave behind their hectic lives.

> ## "One of the best-kept secrets that many tourists overlook!"

Travel Tip...

Reserve one of the three rooms in the front of the Wellesley Hotel facing the river for better access to the summer breeze. Check website below for hotel rates.

>> **ADMISSION:** NO cost to enter the park!

GETTIN' THERE...

75 Miles North of Syracuse, New York, cross the Thousand Islands Bridge on I-81. There is a $2 toll. Take your first exit (exit #51). At the stop sign, go right. This will take you to the state park and Thousand Island Park.

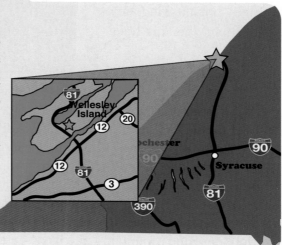

CONTACT...

Call: Lodging/Dining Reservations: (315) 482-3698
Visit: www.wellesley-hotel.com

Adirondack Museum
BLUE MOUNTAIN LAKE, NY

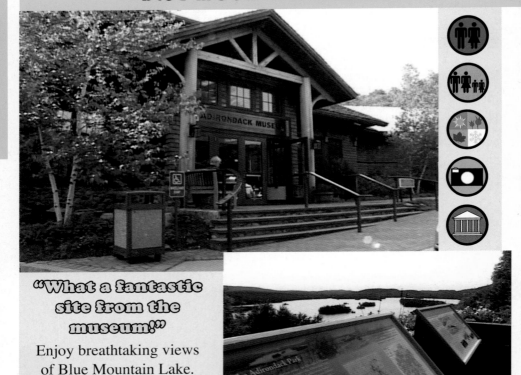

"What a fantastic site from the museum!"

Enjoy breathtaking views of Blue Mountain Lake.

How about a great surprise destination for the whole family? Head high into the Adirondacks to discover a museum that is unlike any you've ever seen before. The Adirondack Museum, north of Old Forge, N.Y. is everything Adirondacks! The huge campus overlooking Blue Mountain Lake has 22 exhibit buildings on 32 beautiful acres. The views from up here are spectacular!

The kids will enjoy this getaway just as much as mom and dad because of the many special activities and programs for families. A 100 year-old, one-room schoolhouse from the Adirondacks is a big eye-opener. So are the many huge, oversized Adirondack chairs you'll find scattered all over the museum grounds. Plan ahead! If you really want to see everything in detail, this getaway could very well take you 2 days to get through!

There is also the Museum Store and Lakeview Café. The Adirondack Museum just celebrated its 50th birthday!

"The kids will enjoy this getaway just as much as mom and dad!"

ATTRACTION...

You can board the luxury rail car "The Oriental", the train that brought the rich and famous to this region long ago.

Travel Tip...

If you really want to take it all in and save some money, buy 1 day's admission and get the 2nd consecutive day free!

ADMISSION: $16 Adults (13+), $8 ages (6-12), Free 5 and under. Discounts for military, students and seniors.

GETTIN THERE...

NYS Thruway exit #31 to Route 12 North. Follow Route 12 to Route 28 through Old Forge, Inlet and Raquette Lake to Blue Mountain Lake. Continue straight through the village to 28N & 30 up the hill about 1 mile. Look for the museum entrance on your left.

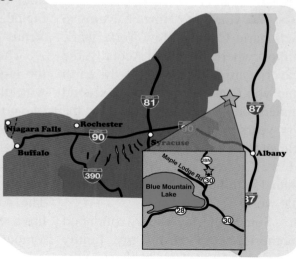

CONTACT...

Hours: Open daily 10am-5pm from late May through mid October. Weekends only in late October.
Call: (518) 352-7311 or **Visit:** www.adkmuseum.org

Howe Caverns
HOWE CAVES, NY

Ready for a 'Journey to the Center of the Earth'? If you go to Howe Caverns in Schoharie County, New York, that's almost where you'll be! Actually, the caverns are 156 feet below the earth and you'll get there by a 32 second underground elevator ride. In the 70 years since the installation of elevators, lighting and walkways, Howe Caverns has welcomed more than 15 million visitors from around the world.

Some of my best childhood memories come from my family getaway to Howe Caverns back in the 60's. Your kids will love it too! And if you want a great way to escape the summer heat, this should do it. Howe Caverns holds a constant 52 degrees, so bring a sweater or a sweatshirt.

The entire underground tour lasts one hour and twenty minutes and even includes a boat ride on "The Lake of Venus".

The operation seems to handle the large summer crowds quite well with plenty of parking and a number of very knowledgeable tour guides. While waiting in line for your tour to begin, you'll see an excellent collection of Howe Caverns memorabilia in their mini-museum. The 300-acre Howe Caverns Estate has a restaurant on the property. Even a motel!

This getaway is a great way to learn about a guy named Lester Howe and his discovery of one of this area's most-visited natural attractions. A perfect getaway for the whole family!

"The caverns are 156 feet below the earth!"

Travel Tip...

Ask about the special 'adult only' Lantern Tours, Friday and Saturday nights by reservation. See Howe Caverns in a different light, the way Lester Howe first saw it in 1842!

- **$27 per person**
- **Ages 16 and up**
- **Reservations necessary**

ADMISSION: Adults (16-64) $18, Seniors (65+) and Ages (12-15) $15, ages (5-11) $10, 4 and under free. 10% AAA discount.

GETTIN THERE...

NYS Thruway to exit #29. Head South on Rt. 10 to Cobleskill, then East on Route 7. Follow the signs to Howe Caverns. Don't get confused when you see signs for another enterprising individual's underground tour. It's Howe Caverns you're looking for.

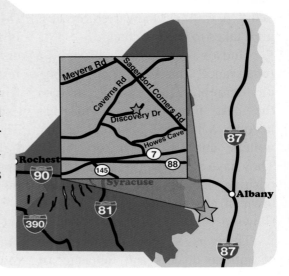

CONTACT...

Hours: Year round, daily 9am-6pm, (winter 9am-5pm) Closed Thanksgiving and Christmas days.

Call: (518) 296-8900 or **Visit:** www.howecaverns.com

Hudson
HUDSON, NY

I t's safe to say Hudson, New York has become a 'small town turnaround' in only a few short years. A walk down Warren Street is all it takes to see the change.

Hudson has gone through a renaissance, thanks in part to big-city entrepreneurs moving in over the past fifteen years. This has become a favorite haunt of artists, writers, antique and history buffs. They have also brought along a fresh, positive, new energy to this small town of about 8,000 people. And it shows!

There is a high concentration of antique dealers and fantastic art galleries all along Warren Street. More than sixty and growing! That's one of the big reasons the new Hudson gets so many visitors. You could spend half the day hitting both sides of the street.

Good food is another big draw... A few of my restaurant discoveries include Ca' Mea, at 333 Warren St. (518) 822-0005 Northern Italian food is what to expect, courtesy of owners Roy and Max. Max also has a restaurant in Cortona, Italy. Lucky for us, he brings his culinary expertise to Hudson, New York! They have just opened Inn at Ca' Mea right next door! www.camearestaurant.com. Like the restaurant, it too is memorable. Room rates $100-$150.

Another gem in town to look for is Olde Hudson at 434 Warren Street. This is one of those gourmet Italian food stores where you can grab a half-pound of sliced Italian salami and a good chunk of provolone cheese to go. Maybe a bottle of imported virgin olive oil too. A touch of New York's Little Italy right in Hudson! (518) 828-6923

"The old is made new again here in Hudson!"

Travel Tip...

On your way out of town, be sure to stop at Olana State Historical Site on Route 9G, the moorish-style villa of Frederick Church. He picked a great location, as you'll see. The view is breathtaking!

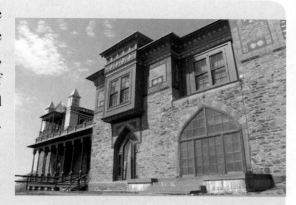

» ADMISSION: FREE!

GETTIN' THERE...

Traveling South on I-87, South of Albany, exit #21 towards Catskill/Rt. 23. Turn left onto CR-23B then a left to get on Rt. 23E. Slight left onto Rt. 23B into Hudson. Hudson is approximately 30 miles South of Albany, N.Y.

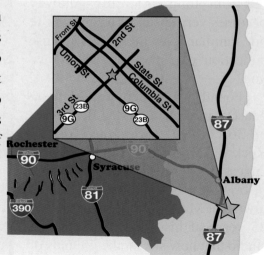

CONTACT...

Call: The Inn at Hudson, 317 Allen Street. (518) 822-9322.
Call: Hudson City B&B, 326 Allen Street. (518) 822-8044.
Call: The Country Squire B&B (518) 822-9229.
Call: Mount Merino Manor B&B (518) 828-5583.

Norman Rockwell Museum
STOCKBRIDGE, MASS.

I
f you remember the famous *Saturday Evening Post* covers from long ago, this getaway becomes very special. Even if you're not familiar with them, this intense collection of Americana will move you.

Found in Stockbridge, Massachusetts in the heart of the Berkshires on 36 colorful acres, the Norman Rockwell Museum houses the world's largest and most significant collection of original Rockwell art. This is the town that Mr. Rockwell spent the last 25 years of his life working in the studio that now sits on the grounds of the museum. They moved it here!

What surprises people most is the size of the original paintings displayed on the museum walls. Most visitors only remember the famous work as it was displayed on magazine covers. All 323 of the original

Saturday Evening Post cover tear sheets featuring each of Norman Rockwell's illustrations from 1916 to 1963 are on display.

Leave your camera in the car! Norman Rockwell Museum does not permit visitors to take still or video photography inside the Museum galleries, and requests that visitors do not carry backpacks or large packages into the galleries.

The Terrace Cafe' along with an extensive gift shop can both be found at the museum.

"This intense collection of Americana will move you."

Travel Tip...

Be sure to see Norman Rockwell's working studio, a big part of the tour. Save your appetite for lunch in the nearby historic New England village of Stockbridge. You'll find a few good restaurants including the historic Red Lion Inn. Try their New England Clam Chowder. Yum!

ADMISSION: $12.50 Adults, $7 College students, Free 18 and under! Parking is free. Audio tours for an additional $5 adults, $4 kids and seniors. Wheelchair accessible.

GETTIN' THERE...

From NYS, exit B3 on the Massachusetts Turnpike onto Rt. 22. Continue South of Rt. 22 to Rt.102 East. Follow through West Stockbridge. Continue on Route 102 East approximately 5.5 miles until you come to a blinking light. Make a right onto Route 183 South. Museum entrance is 0.6 miles down on the left. Follow signs to the Museum.

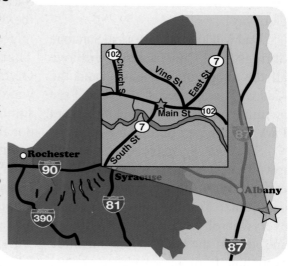

CONTACT...

Hours: Museum open all year round. (except Thanksgiving, Christmas and New Year's Day). **Nov.-April** weekdays 10am-4pm, weekends & holidays 10am-5pm. **May-October & holidays** 10am-5pm. **Studio Tours May-1st week of November** 10am-5pm (not wheelchair accessible).
Call: (413) 298-4100 or **Visit:** www.nrm.org

Saratoga Springs

SARATOGA.NY

It's more than just horse racing! There's something for everyone on this eastern New York Getaway!

Dad will love the historical Saratoga Springs Race Course. Mom will love all the shops on Broadway and the kids will be amazed at the size of the swimming pool at Saratoga Spa State Park. And there's so much more!

Saratoga Springs is a 'walking town' with very wide sidewalks. You can pretty much get to everything on foot. You'll find restaurants everywhere! Shops along Broadway and down the side streets include everything from fine jewelry to oriental rugs and local art work. Late night fun is found on Caroline Street.

Located just south of the town, the sometimes overlooked Saratoga Spa State Park holds an incredible display of classical architecture which makes it a National Historic Landmark. The park holds the nationally known Saratoga Performing Arts Center, the Lincoln Mineral Baths and the incredible Gideon Putnam Hotel. There is also an enormous Olympic-size swimming pool and water slide complex for those hot summer days. Plenty of picnic spot dot the area. Expect to pay a fee to enter certain parts of the park.

Want to spend the night? The Gideon Putnam Hotel is located in Saratoga Spa State Park. Talk about historic! The grandeur and beauty will take your breath away. (800) 732-1560 In town, there are many hotels to choose from. Some of the more traditional hotels, like the Adelphi Hotel, are located right on Broadway which makes easy access to everything this town has to offer.

"You can pretty much get to everything on foot."

Travel Tip...

After a day at the races, it's time to grab something to eat. Two of my favorite restaurants in town are Beverly's for breakfast on Phila Street and for Italian cuisine, the very romantic and cozy family run restaurant Lanci's, 68 Putnam Street near the library. (518) 581-1973.

ADMISSION: FREE! Expect to pay a fee to enter certain parks.

GETTIN' THERE...

From the NYS Thruway, exit #28 towards Fultonville, Route 30A North to Route 29 East. Follow straight into town. Saratoga Springs is just North of Albany, about a 4 hour drive from Rochester.

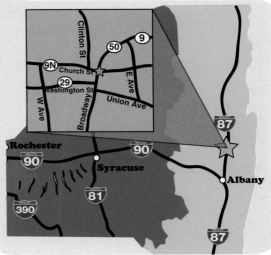

CONTACT...

Call: 1-518-584-3255 or **Visit:** www.saratoga.org
Call: The Gideon Putnam Hotel 1-800-732-1560.

Mirror Lake Inn
77 Mirror Lake Drive
Lake Placid, NY 12946
518-523-2544
www.mirrorlakeinn.com
Lake Placid's only AAA Four-Diamond
lakefront resort, features world-class
dining, luxurious spa services, first class
amenities and magnificent views of
the Adirondack High Peaks.

Morgan Samuels Inn
2920 Smith Road
Canandaigua, NY 14424
585-394-9232
www.morgansamuelsinn.com
The difference between
ordinary and legendary.

Esperanza Mansion
3456 Route 54A
Bluff Point, NY 14478
1-866-927-4400
www.esperanzamansion.com
The mansion offers seven premium over-
sized rooms, and two deluxe rooms. A
bottle of Finger Lakes wine and continental
breakfast are complementary with your stay.

Roycroft Inn
40 South Grove Street
East Aurora, NY 14052
716-652-5552
www.roycroftinn.com
The beauty and history of The
Roycroft Inn can be seen in all 29
guest suites. All are exquisitely
decorated with original and
reproduction Roycroft furnishings

Spend The Night!

19th Green Motel

Route 28
Old Forge, NY 13420
315-369-3575
www.19thgreenmotel.com
Come as a guest...leave as a friend!
Classic Adirondack family-style, all non-smoking 13-unit motel. AAA Approved.

Geneva on the Lake

1001 Lochland Rd, Rt 14
Geneva, N.Y.   14456
315-789-7190
www.genevaonthelake.com
"European Elegance in the Heart of
the Finger Lakes"

Springside Inn

6141 West Lake Rd
Auburn, NY 13021
315-252-7247
www.springsideinn.com
A family owned, 7 guest room country inn
with a 5 bedroom guest house nestled on 13
beautiful acres located across from Owasco
Lake in the Finger Lakes.

Belhurst Castle

4069 Route 14 South
Geneva, NY 14456
315-781-0201
www.belhurst.com
At the heart of Beautiful Belhurst, voted one
of NYS's most romantic places, is a stone
castle built over 100 years ago sitting on the
shores of Seneca Lake. Now expanded into a
luxury hotel, Belhurst offers 47 rooms, fine
dining and award winning Belhurst Winery.

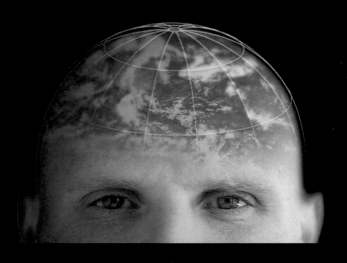

A native of the East Coast, Walter studied at RIT's
School of Photographic Arts & Sciences. His award winning
images have been featured in Archive, Communication Arts,
Graphis, Art Direction Magazine, Print Annual and
Sports Illustrated. Walter's artistry has been hired by
major corporations and ad agencies both local and national.
As a commercial photographer his client list is second
to none. Personal and portrait photography are
also part of his repertoire.

WALTER COLLEY

IMAGES

Walter Colley Images, Inc
174 Griffith Street
Rochester, NY 14607
www.waltercolleyimages.com
585.461.4090

Esperanza Mansion

DINING & SIGHTSEEING
THE ESPERANZA ROSE

*E*SCAPE TO COMFORTABLE ELEGANCE

*E*XCEPTIONAL ACCOMMODATIONS

*E*XTRAORDINARY DINING

*G*RAND BALLROOM & TERRACE

*W*EDDINGS - MEETINGS - EVENTS

*B*REATHTAKING LAKE VIEWS

*F*INGER LAKES WINE COUNTRY

*E*SPERANZA ROSE SPRING, SUMMER
AND FALL CRUISES DAILY

56 ROUTE 54A, BLUFF POINT, NY 14478   1.866.927.4400
WWW.ESPERANZAMANSION.COM

IN THE PROCESS OF MAKING YOUR BUSINESS FAMOUS,
YOU HAVE TO SHAKE THINGS UP.

A FULL SERVICE ADVERTISING AGENCY

WWW.EARTHQUAKEGROUP.COM

iMAGINATIVE > iNNOVATIVE > iNVENTIVE

FOR ALL YOUR DESIGN NEEDS

GRAPHIC DESIGN
WEB DESIGN
PHOTOGRAPHY
AND MORE

WWW.SX2DESIGN.COM

NOTES!

Check'em off as you go! Log on to www.TheGetawayGuy.com and send Mike an email when you visit all fifty getaways. Where'd you go? Who'd you go with? Who do you know that would love each getaway? What was your favorite part of the trip? Memorable restaurants? Other details?

———

———

———

———

———

———

———

———

———

———

———

———

———

———

———

———

———

———

———

———

———

———

———

———

———

———

———

———

———

NOTES!

Check'em off as you go! Log on to www.TheGetawayGuy.com and send Mike an email when you visit all fifty getaways. Where'd you go? Who'd you go with? Who do you know that would love each getaway? What was your favorite part of the trip? Memorable restaurants? Other details?

NOTES!

Check'em off as you go! Log on to www.TheGetawayGuy.com and send Mike an email when you visit all fifty getaways. Where'd you go? Who'd you go with? Who do you know that would love each getaway? What was your favorite part of the trip? Memorable restaurants? Other details?

_____
_____
_____
_____
_____
_____
_____
_____
_____
_____
_____
_____
_____
_____
_____
_____
_____
_____
_____
_____
_____
_____
_____
_____
_____
_____
_____
_____
_____

NOTES!

Check'em off as you go! Log on to www.TheGetawayGuy.com and send Mike an email when you visit all fifty getaways. Where'd you go? Who'd you go with? Who do you know that would love each getaway? What was your favorite part of the trip? Memorable restaurants? Other details?

NOTES!

Check'em off as you go! Log on to www.TheGetawayGuy.com and send Mike an email when you visit all fifty getaways. Where'd you go? Who'd you go with? Who do you know that would love each getaway? What was your favorite part of the trip? Memorable restaurants? Other details?

_____

_____

_____

_____

_____

_____

_____

_____

_____

_____

_____

_____

_____

_____

_____

_____

_____

_____

_____

_____

_____

_____

_____

_____

_____

_____

_____

_____

NOTES!

Check'em off as you go! Log on to www.TheGetawayGuy.com and send Mike an email when you visit all fifty getaways. Where'd you go? Who'd you go with? Who do you know that would love each getaway? What was your favorite part of the trip? Memorable restaurants? Other details?

NOTES!

Check'em off as you go! Log on to www.TheGetawayGuy.com and send Mike an email when you visit all fifty getaways. Where'd you go? Who'd you go with? Who do you know that would love each getaway? What was your favorite part of the trip? Memorable restaurants? Other details?

_____
_____
_____
_____
_____
_____
_____
_____
_____
_____
_____
_____
_____
_____
_____
_____
_____
_____
_____
_____
_____
_____
_____
_____
_____
_____
_____
_____

NOTES!

Check'em off as you go! Log on to www.TheGetawayGuy.com and send Mike an email when you visit all fifty getaways. Where'd you go? Who'd you go with? Who do you know that would love each getaway? What was your favorite part of the trip? Memorable restaurants? Other details?

_____
_____
_____
_____
_____
_____
_____
_____
_____
_____
_____
_____
_____
_____
_____
_____
_____
_____
_____
_____
_____
_____
_____
_____
_____
_____

NOTES!

Check'em off as you go! Log on to www.TheGetawayGuy.com and send Mike an email when you visit all fifty getaways. Where'd you go? Who'd you go with? Who do you know that would love each getaway? What was your favorite part of the trip? Memorable restaurants? Other details?

_____
_____
_____
_____
_____
_____
_____
_____
_____
_____
_____
_____
_____
_____
_____
_____
_____
_____
_____
_____
_____
_____
_____
_____
_____
_____
_____
_____
_____
_____
_____